200 Years of Glass:

A History of Libbey Glass

By Robert Zollweg

UNIVERSITY OF TOLEDO PRESS

The University of Toledo Press

Toledo, Ohio

2019

The University of Toledo Press

www.utoledopress.com

Copyright 2019

By The University of Toledo Press

200 Years of Glass:

A History of Libbey Glass

By Robert Zollweg

ISBN 978-1-7332664-0-6

Edited by Yarko Kuk

Project assistance from Abby Byers, Erin Czerniak, Barbara L. Floyd, and Julie McMaster.

Book design by Yarko Kuk

Cover photo: Photo by Valentino Sarra. It features Nick Schiel making an object called Cornucopia, from Libbey's Modern American Series.

Dedication

This book is dedicated to

John Meier

1947 – 2017

and to all past and current employees for making Libbey what it is today.

Table of Contents

Acknowledgements

This book would not have been possible without the gracious and unending assistance, support, and counsel of a group of dedicated historians, archivists, librarians, and Libbey devotees. Special thanks to Julie McMaster and Barbara Floyd.

Thanks also to the Toledo Museum of Art; Anthony Tscherne, Gary Raschke, and Sandy Shultz of Libbey Glass; Sara Mouch and The University of Toledo Ward M. Canaday Center for Special Collections; Suzanne Abrams Rebillard and the Corning Museum of Glass; Laura Voelz and the Toledo-Lucas County Public Library's Local History Department; Sarah Kozma and the Onondaga Historical Association; Matthew Weickert and the Wallaceburg and District Museum; Dorothy Schofield and Katie Campbell and the Sandwich Glass Museum; Jessica Whitehead and the Kentucky Derby Museum; and the staff of the Ojai Valley Museum.

Perhaps most importantly, this author would like to acknowledge the incalculable contributions of the thousands and thousands of Libbey Glass employees over two centuries. Their commitment to manufacturing, design, and innovation helped make Libbey one of the premier names in the glass industry. Without their contributions, Libbey would not be one of the world's leaders in glass.

Robert Zollweg

Robert Zollweg

Introduction

In 2018, Libbey celebrated its 200th anniversary, a significant milestone few American companies have achieved. Throughout my career in the glass industry, and, in more recent years, as Chairman and CEO of Libbey, I have had the honor to witness first-hand the types of people and innovations that have enabled this company to survive, and thrive, for two centuries.

In *200 Years of Glass*, Robert shares stories of some of the stand-out characters, pivotal decisions, and iconic designs that have helped shaped Libbey's 200-year legacy. Robert, himself, has dedicated more than 40 years to Libbey, leading product design and innovation. He is well respected in his field, in the glass industry, and in our community. His knowledge and passion for Libbey and innovation are evident throughout this book and make him uniquely qualified to share Libbey's history in this pictorial reference.

While this book looks at the first 200 years of Libbey, we are celebrating more than our legacy. As a company, we are looking ahead to where our heritage of innovation poises us to venture next. Make no mistake, we are not finished innovating the way people experience everyday moments. We are just getting started.

Cheers to each of you, to *200 Years of Glass*, and more importantly, to what's next!

William A. Foley
Chairman
Libbey Inc.

William A. Foley

Chapter 1 – The 1800s

The New England Glass Company

Libbey Glass, Toledo's first and oldest glass manufacturing operation and a company that pioneered more than a century of innovations in the glass industry, can trace its roots back to 1818 to East Cambridge, Massachusetts.

New England industrialist Deming Jarves, along with associates Amos Binney, Daniel Hastings, and Edmund H. Monroe, incorporated the New England Glass Company on February 16, 1818.[1] The "father of the American glass industry," Jarves got his start in the business in 1809 when he and a group of other investors purchased Boston Crown Glass.[2]

Following the War of 1812, England flooded the market with cheap glass products, forcing many glass companies, including Boston Crown Glass, into bankruptcy. In 1814, Jarves found a new group of investors to rescue Boston Crown Glass. The firm was renamed Boston Porcelain and Glass, but it struggled against a variety of economic and material challenges before it too failed.[3]

Facing page: [Fig. 1-1] A New England Glass Works display at an industrial fair, sometime between 1880 and 1888.

In 1818 Jarves' latest venture, the New England Glass Company, acquired the former Boston Porcelain and Glass manufacturing facility at the northeast corner of North and Water Streets in East Cambridge to house the new business.[4]

The glassmaking process of the early 1800s was time consuming, with much done by hand. Workers needed years of practice to develop the necessary skills to manufacture, cut, and polish glass. All of these factors combined to make glass a costly luxury rather than the basic household product it is today.

In 1826, Thomas H. Leighton, a skilled glassworker from England who

Deming Jarves

has been credited with "re-discovering" the process used to make ruby glass,[5] was hired as the factory's superintendent. The following year, the New England Glass Company introduced pressed glass. By 1830, the company had more than 150 employees and produced 25,000 pounds of glass per week.

New England Glass manufactured both blown

A pair of pieces manufactured by the New England Glass Company. Below: [Fig. 1-2] A large compote featuring a tightly scalloped rim and 327 flowers made sometime between 1860 and 1877. Right: [Fig. 1-3] A large water pitcher engraved with grapes and leaves, possibly by Louis Vaupel, around 1875.

and pressed glass. In 1850 Jarves hired another skilled engraver, German native Louis Vaupel, who would later become head of design and engraving at the company.[6] At the same time, one of Jarves' other glassmaking firms, Jarves and Commeraise, of South Boston, Massachusetts, hired an up and coming 23-year-old to serve as Jarves' corporate clerk. That man was William L. Libbey.

In addition to New England Glass, Jarves had three other major glass manufacturing companies: Boston Sandwich, Mount Washington Glass Works, and Cape Cod Glass.

During his tenure with Jarves and Commeraise, Libbey became one of the firm's most trusted employees, having access to manufacturing methods and recipes, knowledge of shipping, importing, and exporting.

William L. Libbey

By 1860, Libbey had been named co-manager of Mount Washington Glass. He and a master glass blower subsequently purchased the company in 1866. Under Libbey's guidance, Mount Washington Glass Works flourished and soon expanded oper-

Right: [Fig. 1-4] A deep blue lead glass made by the New England Glass Company, engraved with "Father's Gift to Maria 1860."

Left: [Fig. 1-5] A cut and gilded vase blown from four layers of glass by William Leighton at the New England Glass Company, between 1848 and 1858.

ations to New Bedford, Massachusetts. It was in 1869 that Libbey introduced his 15-year-old son, Edward Drummond Libbey, to the glass business. In 1870, following the death of Jarves, the elder Libbey was named general manager of the New England Glass Company,[7] marking the start of 55 years of direct Libbey family involvement in one of the foremost glass companies of the era.

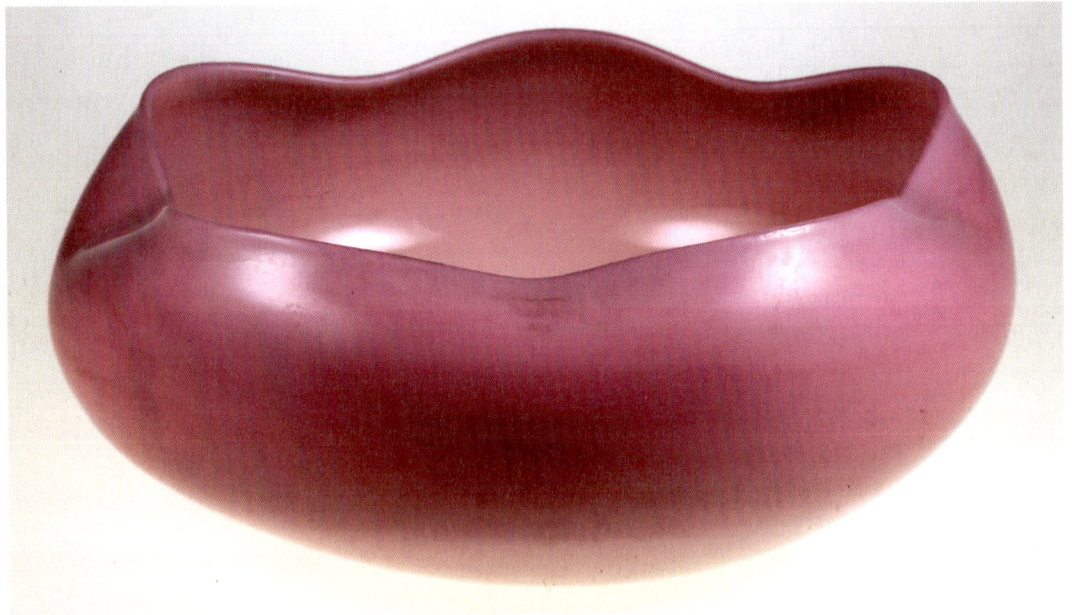

Above: [Fig. 1-6] A Wild Rose glass bowl manufactured by New England Glass Works between 1886 and 1888.

Facing page, left: [Fig. 1-7] A goblet engraved by Louis Vaupel between 1865 and 1875.

Facing page, right: [Fig. 1-8] An Amberina pitcher, the entire body of which has been cut in the hobstar pattern, between 1886 and 1888.

When Libbey took the helm of New England Glass the business was struggling, as were many other glass companies in the region. Commercially, they had peaked in 1850, and over the next twenty years, the center of the glass industry in America had shifted to western Pennsylvania and West Virginia, where coal, a cheaper fuel, was plentiful.[8]

Tough economic times in the early 1870s coupled with a declining market share put New England Glass in a precarious position. In 1874, Libbey hired his 20-year-old son, Edward, as a clerk with the company. The company gained considerable fame with its note-worthy display at the 1876 Centennial Exhibition in Philadelphia – thanks in large part to the extraordinary designs of craftsman Louis Vaupel – but it was a losing struggle, and in 1877 the New England Glass Company was forced to close its doors.

After efforts to sell the plant were unsuccessful, Libbey leased the plant and opened New England Glass Works, Wm. L. Libbey and Son Proprietors, in 1878. In 1880, with his son fully involved in the venture, William made Edward a partner in the business and renamed the company William L. Libbey and Son.[9]

The Libbeys expanded and introduced remarkable examples of colored glass, including Pomona, Amberina, Peachglow, and Agata. These new

Left: [Fig. 1-9] Vase maufactured by New England Glass Works, around 1885. Probably etched and engraved by Joseph Locke.

products, developed by Joseph Locke, a craftsman hired by Edward Libbey[10], significantly changed the financial positioning of the new company. Sales of these lines helped the company stave off bankruptcy in 1883.[11] In that same year, William Libbey died unexpectedly and full control of the company fell to his son Edward. The business was still in serious financial difficulties, and the powerful American Flint Glass Workers Union was threatening a strike

Above: [Fig. 1-10] A Pomona glass bowl, above, made by the New England Glass Works about 1885.

Right: [Fig. 1-11] A Maize glass pitcher, right, made by the W.L. Libbey and Son Glass Company around 1890.

for better wages. When the strike was called in early 1888, Libbey knew he had to take drastic action to save the company and his financial future. He closed the plant in East Cambridge and set out to find a suitable new location outside of Massachusetts.

"We will be true, loyal, honest citizens of Toledo"

The city of Toledo was incorporated in 1837 as result of the merger of a pair of neighboring settlements, Port Lawrence and Vistula. Within 50 years, the city boasted a population in excess of 50,000. Situated on the banks of the Maumee River where it flows into Lake Erie, Toledo served as a grain and coal distribution point and a transportation hub. While the city had a variety of industries, civic leaders were determined to identify a catalyst to help Toledo become "the great industrial metropolis of the West."[12]

The "Business Men's Committee" was founded in April 1887 in an effort to help Toledo capitalize on the recent natural gas boom in Findlay, Ohio, a community 40 miles south of Toledo. William H. Maher was elected secretary of the group. Maher "personally contacted dozens of manufacturers across the country" in an effort to get them to consider relocating to Toledo. He sent out thousands of mailers to a variety of industries "with special emphasis on those with heat-intensive operations like steel and glass manufacturing."[13]

Edward Libbey was one of more than two dozen entrepreneurs who responded to Maher's solicitations. Between 1886 and 1890, more than 100 glass houses opened within a 25-mile radius of Findlay.[14] Libbey bucked the trend and instead picked Toledo as the home for his future factory.

After multiple visits to the area, Libbey decided on Toledo for a number of reasons. In addition to the lure of cheap natural gas, the abundance of high silica sand, and access to the Maumee River waterway to the Great Lakes, Libbey gravitated to Toledo because of the city's public school system, professional fire department, water service, and large pool of skilled workers and young boys who would be needed to staff the new facility.[15]

Libbey was lured to northwest Ohio on the news of plentiful natural gas supplies, but Toledo's role as one of the nation's foremost railroad centers helped him make up his mind. When Libbey visited Toledo in 1887, more than 140 passenger trains arrived in and departed from Toledo each day. More than 20 railroad lines served the city, and Toledo handled as much grain as Chicago.[16] The rail lines afforded quick and easy access to coal from Pittsburgh and oil from Cleveland, giving Libbey and his new facility access to multiple cheap fuel sources.[17]

Having settled on Toledo as the future home of his glass company, Libbey needed land, and he turned to the city to provide it. Four acres of land – roughly bordered by Ash Street to the west, Buckeye Street to the east, Champlain Street to the south, and the Wheeling & Lake Erie Railroad to the north – were identified as the site of the new factory. The *Toledo Blade* described the site as:

a handsome knoll of ground which rises just where Ash and Buckeye streets cross the Wheeling & Lake Erie tracks. The ground consists of four acres, and nature evidently intended the spot for a glass works. Search the world over and you cannot find a bet-

ter location. When Mr. George Pomeroy first showed Mr. Libbey the spot he was charmed with the site.[18]

Owned by the Bissell and Collins families, the city sought pledges from area businesses and individuals to raise the $4,000 needed to purchase the parcels. By February 1888, more than 230 individu-

S. O. RICHARDSON JR. SECTY.　　　　　E. D. LIBBEY, PRES. & TREAS.　　　　　JOS. LOCKE, SUPT.

The W. L. Libbey & Son Company,

NEW ENGLAND GLASS WORKS.

Manufacturers of

FINEST QUALITY CUT AND ARTISTIC GLASSWARE.

SALESROOMS.
155 FRANKLIN ST. BOSTON.
18 COLLEGE PLACE NEW YORK.
19 WABASH AVE. CHICAGO.
FACTORY, TOLEDO, O.

Toledo, O. _____ 2/14/88. _____ 188

Gentlemen;—
　　　　　The total amount thus far subscribed towards paying for the site for the Libbey Glass Works is $3488.
　　　　　We need $512 more to make up the necessary amount to pay for the four (4) acres. Please sign the amount you will contribute towards this enterprise below.

A.M.Woolson.	$25.00	J.T.Newton.	$25.00
Frank Roff.	10.00	John Berdan.	28.75
Barfield & Atkin.	10.00	Daudt Glass & Crockery Co.	28.75
T.J.Collins.	5.00	J.N.Mockett.	25.00

Know All Men by these Presents:

THAT I Edward D. Libbey

in consideration of *Five Thousand Dollars*

to me paid by *The W. L. Libbey & Son Company*

the receipt whereof is hereby acknowledged, do hereby GRANT, BARGAIN, SELL AND CONVEY to the said

The W. L. Libbey and Son Company;

its successors heirs and assigns forever, All that part of Block number two (2) in the Bissell Farm addition to the City of Toledo, Lucas County, Ohio described as follows; to wit: —

Commencing in the centre of Ash street extended at a point S 33.25 feet Northwesterly from a stone monument in the centre of Ash and Michigan Streets, (which point is in the Northwesterly line of the Wheeling and Lake Erie Railroad Company's Right of Way) thence Northwesterly along said centre line of Ash street extended 275.75 feet; thence Northeasterly on a line parallel with Michigan street S 73/3 feet to the Northwesterly corner of land conveyed to The Toledo Window Glass Company; thence Southeasterly on a line parallel with said centre line of Ash street, extended 319.25 feet to said Wheeling and Lake Erie Railroad Company's Right of Way; thence Southwesterly along said Right of Way to the place of beginning containing

als and businesses had pledged $3,488 toward the $4,000 goal. Pledges came from local banks and natural gas companies, including Northwest Natural Gas Company, Toledo Natural Gas Company, Northern National Bank, Second National Bank, and Merchant National Bank.

Other business donors included Daudt Glass and Crockery Company, Bostwick Braun and Company, Meilink Furniture Company, Lenk Wine Company, Toledo Brewing Company, Woolson Spice Company, Lasalle and Koch, Smith Bridge Company, the *Toledo Bee*, the *Toledo Blade*, Vulcan Iron Works, Moreton Truck Company, Pearl Steam Laundry, and the Toledo Pump Company.

Individual businessmen also stepped up, and the February 1888 pledge memo included names of many prominent Toledoans, including Woolson, Collins, Berdan, Ketcham, Douglass, Walbridge, Eaton, Secor, Conant, Hallet, Milburn, Dority, Root, Sawyer, and Scott.

By the spring of 1888, the city had purchased the land and ground had been broken for the new factory. Edward Libbey purchased the land from the city on April 5, 1888 for $4,000, and just over two months later, on June 23, Libbey sold the land to his business – the W.L. Libbey and Son Company – for $5,000.

In addition to the land for the factory, the city gave Libbey 50 lots on nearby streets in Glassboro

Left: The warranty deed dated June 23, 1888, in which Edward Libbey sold the land to the W.L. Libbey & Son Company for $5,000.

16

to build housing for the new glass workers. Most of these small homes still exist today, many having been altered and remodeled over the years.

The move to Toledo was as monumental for the company as it would end up being for the city. A century before Toledo was known world over as "The Glass Capital of the World," the *Toledo Blade* devoted an unprecedented three full columns of space in the Saturday, August 18, 1888 evening edition to document the arrival of Libbey and hundreds of workers to Toledo the day before. The paper proclaimed:

> From Boston to Boss-town.
> From the Hub of the East to the Hub of the West.
> From the City by the Sea to the City of the Lakes.
> From the Land of Classical Culture to the Land of Natural Gas.
> All Toledo welcomes you to the future glass center of the world.
> Yesterday the employees of the Libbey Glass works removed from Boston to To-ledo; to-day they are setting in their new homes and putting things to rights in the factory, and Monday the Libbey Glass works will be in full blast.[19]

Hundreds of Toledoans turned out to welcome the train carrying 115 workers and their families to Toledo. The new arrivals were "treated to an ovation, which fairly carried off their breath. The

Above: [Fig. 1-13] One of the homes Libbey employees built in the neighborhood adjacent to the new plant.

first thing that they heard was the strains of Tony Leon's [Grand Army of the Republic] band, and then followed cheers from the Toledo citizens and workmen already in the city."[20]

From the train station in the Middle Grounds, the Libbey contingent proceeded to march to the site of the new factory. News accounts described the procession as "presenting an imposing appearance. A colony of 500 men added to a city is an event which does not happen every day, even in natural gas cities. The effect of the parade was not lost upon the businessmen of Toledo, many of whom gathered at the doors out of curiosity and interest. Bells were ringing, whistles were blowing, and everybody indulged in a general jubilee."[21]

Upon arriving at the site of the new factory, the Libbey employees and their families:

found a tempting supper prepared by Toledo citizens, and spread upon tables placed upon the green. Just at the close of the day a beautiful sunset illuminated the entire

"BOSS-TOWN!"

That's What the Libbey Glass Workers Call Toledo.

This City Suits Them, and Why Shouldn't It?

RIGHT ROYAL RECEPTION

Given the Kings of Kings Upon Their Entrance to Toledo.

The Libbey Glass Works Ready to Start Up With 500 Men.

From Boston to Boss-town.
From the Hub of the East to the Hub of

loyal, honest citizens of Toledo. And now, Mayor Hamilton, I desire to present to you the first piece of glass blown in Toledo. It is made from Toledo sand and the fuel was that wonderful and powerful agent, natural gas.

When Mr Libbey referred to the employes being ready to promise to be true citizens of Toledo he was intercepted by cheers and cries of "We are. We are showing that the best of feeling exists between employer and employed.

Mayor Hamilton on behalf of the city of Toledo accepted the gift of a cylinder of glass stating that it was indeed an offering most valuable.

MR. CHASE

was then called out and introduced as the gentleman who was responsible for the first glass blown in Toledo. He thanked the audience, stated that he could blow glass better than he could make speeches and disappeared.

REYNOLD VOIT.

There were loud calls for Reynold Voit when the cheers for Mr. Libby, loud and long continued, died away. He stated that it was indeed difficult for people to realize how hard it was to tear away from the old home, the old associations, the old interests, but the men knew only this, that they were coming to a strange land, that they would have the same kind and good master that they had in the East. He was glad to receive such a royal welcome.

MR. J. R. KELLOCH.

Mr. J. R. Kelloch was next called for. He stated that although iron is king, glassworkers are kings of kings, and urged his fellow workmen to be honest and true, and stated there was no reason why the worker in glass should not take a position high in

ledo society. He is said by experts to have a voice equal to any in that city of culture and music. He is a fine baritone singer. He is unmarried. Already he has been invited to give a concert by his new friends in this city. He is also a member of the Commonwealth quartette of Boston.

"THE GAFFER."

John Hopkins, the "Gaffer," or the floor manager, as this term is known among all the glass men, is another Boston man, born and bred. He was 50 years of age last Sunday, is married and has a daughter who is known and recognized as one of the leading sopranos of Boston. She is at present at Augusta, Me., spending a portion of the summer. She will complete next year a past graduate course at the Boston Conservatory of Music, and will then come to Toledo, where she will be welcome.

WILLIAM F. DONOVAN.

William F. Donovan, the cashier and book-keeper has been with Mr. Libbey for ten years. He is a Boston boy, and is universally pronounced the right man in the right place.

WILLIE ANDERSON.

Willie Anderson, the foreman of the glass cutting department is one of the best glass cutters in the trade. He is a Scotchman by birth, an American by adoption, and a jolly good fellow when you know him. He learned his trade with Libbey, and has won his way to the front by hard work and close application. His family comes with him from the East to make their home in this city. He was a successful competitor for a prize for the best and most artistic design in cut glass awarded in Boston last year.

ED. JEWETT.

West, and the scenery, ever beautiful at this point in Lower Town, was lighted up with a glow, glory and grandeur truly magnificent while the immense factory, with the American flag floating to the breeze presented a picture worth traveling far to see. The tired pilgrims who had found here a New Beulah land were invited to assume charge of the refreshments and responded with a will.[22]

Libbey himself addressed the gathered citizenry proclaiming:

Had I all eloquence, I could scarcely do justice to the occasion. Coming, as we do, from Massachusetts to Ohio, we are met here in such a spirit that all dread has dispersed and all reluctance disappeared. I wish I could find words to express our thanks to the people of Toledo to-night for this royal welcome. We want to say upon the very threshold of our arrival that we have come to stay. And we will promise you, Mr. Mayor, and the people of Toledo, that we will be true, loyal, honest citizens of Toledo.[23]

While August 17 was the day celebrated by residents and workers alike, hundreds of other Libbey employees and their families had arrived in the city in the weeks and months before. The new factory cost in excess of $50,000, and was stocked with 50 carloads of machinery – valued at $25,000 – that

Above: [Fig. 1-14] The interior of a kiln at the new factory.

19

had been shipped in from Massachusetts.[24] According to press reports:

> The furnace, factory, engine house, boiler shed, engine room, acid and kiln building, storage sheds occupy a ground floor away and apart from the main building, the entire space aggregating 1,500,000 space enclosed.

> The factory has been built in the latest and most approved manner, almost fire proof and constructed with especial view to the comfort and convenience of the men, and is considered by the builder, the architect and others familiar with the building to be the best on the continent.

> The floor space in the factory is divided as follows: first floor – packing, etching shops and offices; second floor – decorating room; and third floor – cutting shops.[25]

Right: [Fig. 1-18] A three-part glass lamp made by the W.L. Libbey and Son Glass Company around 1892. The globe features the Ellsmere pattern.

Inside the new Libbey plant shortly after it opened in 1888. Facing page, left: [Fig. 1-15] The mold room. Facing page, right: [Fig. 1-16]: Engravers at work. Below: [Fig. 1-17] Craftsmen shape blanks.

The new factory boasted a 13-pot furnace with a capacity of 16 tons of molten glass. It produced its first piece of glass less than a week later, on August 22, 1888.[26]

Above: [Fig. 1-20] An Amberina glass tumbler.

Right: [Fig. 1-21] Edward Libbey in his office at the new factory.

Facing page: [Fig. 1-19] The new Libbey plant shortly after opening in 1888.

Innovation, Exposition, and Michael Owens

Despite the fanfare surrounding the arrival of the new enterprise, within months there were problems with the new factory and operations at the plant "would turn out to be a nightmare."[27] The new furnace was defective, production speeds and quality levels were far below company standards, and many of the workers who made the trip to Toledo ended up disliking "the Midwestern living environment (and) returned to the more cosmopolitan Boston area."[28] These were difficult times, but Libbey was determined to survive and make a successful glass company. While Libbey lacked the requisite management skills, "finance, investment, marketing, and recruiting were his strengths."[29]

With all the problems at the new factory, Libbey needed to hire additional workers. In his search for skilled glassblowers, he traveled to what was then the glass center of the country – Pennsylvania and West Virginia. Libbey hired many qualified men; one of them was a 29-year-old named Michael J. Owens. During their first meeting in West Virginia "Libbey saw a positive, hard-driving man, not common in the glass industry."[30]

Owens started in Toledo as a glassblower, but was named plant superintendent a short time later.[31] He took over a plant that was "in disarray," plagued with lazy workers and continuing issues with the furnace. "Discipline was lacking, as workers drank hard to relieve their homesickness and work problems."[32]

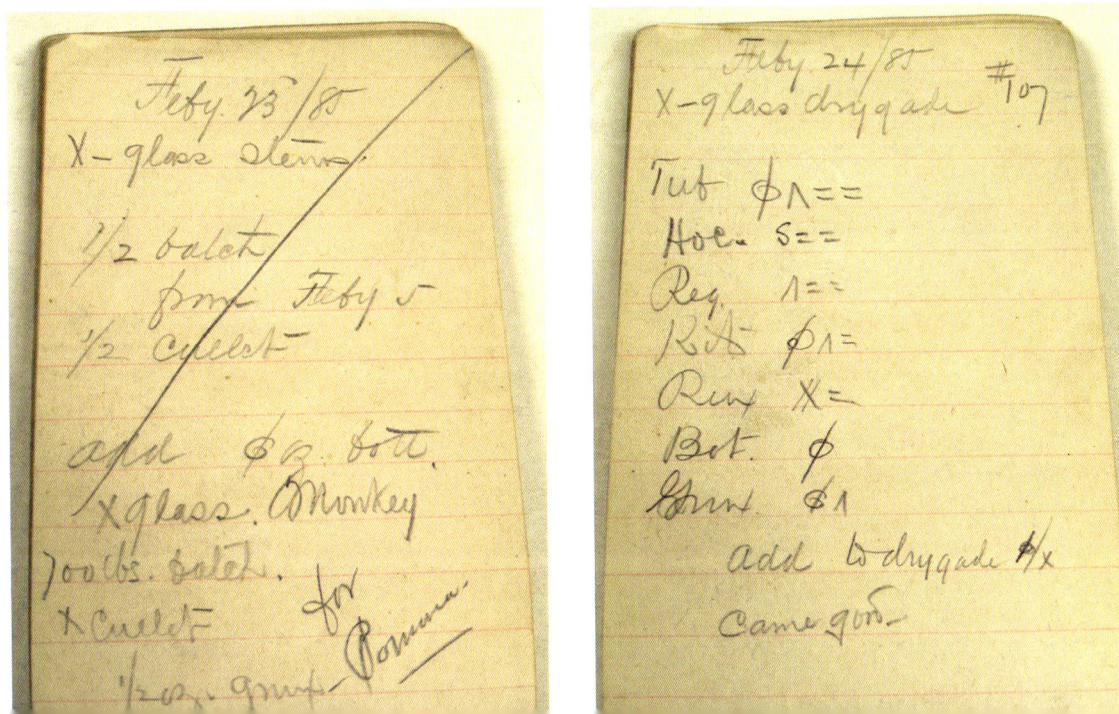

Left: [Fig. 1-22] Two pages, dated February 1885, from one of Edward Libbey's batch books. The books are small notebooks with glass recipes and other production notes.

Facing page: [Fig. 1-23] Libbey Glass workers in 1890. Notice the number of young boys who worked at the plant alongside the craftsmen.

Owens promptly fired many employees without informing Libbey. When Libbey arrived at work the following morning and found the factory quiet, he questioned Owens, but ultimately trusted the new superintendent's decision. Owens' strategy worked. He rehired workers who were motivated and wanted the job. Libbey saw this success and soon placed him in charge of every aspect of production at the plant.

Left: [Fig. 1-24] The Washington Glass Works display at the 1876 Centennial Exhibition.

While Owens worked hard to get the Toledo plant on the right track, the company's financial future remained uncertain. Things changed in 1890, when a golden opportunity arose for Libbey and his factory.

Corning Glass Works in Corning, New York was having labor problems and was unable to fulfill its contract with Edison General Electric for incandescent light bulbs. Libbey was subsequently awarded the contract to make the bulbs. He rented an idle glass factory in Findlay, Ohio to produce the light bulbs. This venture marked a turn in Libbey's fortunes.[33] Profits soared. Along the way, Owens experimented with semi-automated blowing equipment to speed up production and eliminate some of the child labor force. In 1892, a new 10-pot furnace was added at the Toledo plant and the electric light bulb production moved to Toledo. That same year, the company changed its name to the Libbey Glass Company.

In 1876, two years after his father hired him to work at New England Glass, Edward Libbey made one of the most formative business trips of his young career. The 22-year-old joined his father at the 1876 Centennial Exhibition in Philadelphia. Close to 10 million people attended the expo, which celebrated the 100th anniversary of the Declaration of Independence. New England Glass was one of a number of glass companies with a presence at the exposition. One of the most popular exhibits at the exposition was a working glasshouse operated by Gillinder & Son. Guests were treated to demonstrations of pressed glass and could purchase a variety of souvenir pieces. The Gillinder & Sons' exhibit was wildly successful, attracting large crowds and earning the company many accolades. It also stoked Edward Libbey's desire to take his company to the fair in 1893.[34]

A skilled promoter, Libbey saw the 1893 World's Columbian Exposition in Chicago as an unparalleled opportunity to promote the Libbey Glass Company. He proposed constructing a temporary 10-pot exhibit that would be staffed by skilled workers from Toledo.[35] Libbey Company executives Sol Richardson, Bill Donovan, and Jefferson Robinson, Sr. "vigorously opposed" the idea of participating in the 1893 Exposition.[36] Robinson said the company lacked the financial resources for such an initiative, and while Libbey owned more than 50 percent of the company's stock, "he was still dependent on full cooperation from the board."[37]

The board ended up authorizing $50,000 for the project, far less than the $250,000 Libbey estimated was needed. Toledo banker John Ketcham pledged $100,000, and Libbey was able to raise the remaining $100,000. The Libbey Glass Company

The Libbey Glass pavilion at the World's Columbian Exposition of 1893. Top: [Fig. 1-25] The pavilion under construction. Right: [Fig. 1-26] The furnace inside the pavilion.

of Illinois was formed for the endeavor. Mr. Libbey was going to the fair.

The 1893 World's Columbian Exposition was a massive event. It covered more than 1,000 acres[38] and attracted more than 27 million guests.[39] Vendors at the exposition introduced new products to the public, including the Ferris wheel, Pabst Beer, Aunt Jemima syrup, Cream of Wheat, Juicy Fruit gum, hamburgers, and soda pop.[40]

Located on the midway between Washington and Jackson parks, Libbey had grand ideas for his company's exhibit. He hired Toledo architect David L. Stine, the "Dean" of Toledo architects, to design the Italianate pavilion:[41]

> [It] was to be a fully functional glasshouse producing Bohemian and Venetian art glass. The palace was designed to hold 2,000 visitors. Its entrance would be flanked by twin towers and topped with a 100-foot dome (which was actually a chimney). … Libbey would sell paperweights, cut-glass tableware, doorstops, candy-striped canes, and fair souvenirs.[42]

To make his grand vision a reality, Libbey turned to Owens to manage the venture, and Owens did not disappoint. Fueled by Ohio oil,[43] the pavilion

Top: [Fig. 1-27] Craftsmen making glass thread.

Left: [Fig. 1-28] Women use a loom to weave together silk and the glass thread to make fabric.

was up and running for the exposition's opening day on May 1, 1893.

Visitors to the Libbey pavilion received a spun glass bow on the end of a stickpin. The spun glass was developed by Herman Hammesjahr, a craftsman Libbey brought in from Germany. Hammesjahr's spun glass was combined with silk to make a material that could be used to fashion necklaces, napkins, and dresses.[44]

Georgia Cayvan, a famous Broadway actress of the day, saw a lampshade made from spun glass fabric on display at the pavilion and requested a dress be made for her out of the fabric. Libbey saw the huge marketing potential of such a dress and had one made for the actress and a second made for display at the fair.

When Princess Eulalia of Spain visited the Libbey Glass pavilion, she was so taken by the dress that she requested one be made for her. In great ceremony, Libbey presented the dress to the princess and received a certificate naming the Libbey Glass Company the official "Glass Cutters to Her Royal Highness Infanta Dona Eulalia of Spain."[45]

Joseph Rosenberger, "Libbey's best gaffer," developed several new cut glass patterns at the exposition and won the exhibition's gold medal for cut glass. The expo closed on October 30, 1893. More than 2 million people had visited the Libbey pavilion,[46] and revenue from admission fees and sales of souvenirs and other products made the

Right: [Fig. 1-29] A Libbey glass dress displayed on a manequin.

venture a roaring success. After repaying the initial $250,000, Libbey still made a $100,000 profit[47] and was able to pay "a considerable dividend to the shareholders."[48]

Libbey Glass continued to benefit from its presence at the exposition long after the event had ended. Libbey gained an international reputation for brilliant cut glass. "Sales increased for years after the fair and an active foreign market was created. The Libbey trademark was known throughout the world."[49] Despite the recession of 1893 to 1898, Libbey Glass turned profits that allowed it to pay dividends of 40 to 100 percent.[50]

After the exposition, Michael Owens returned to Toledo. He was tasked with managing the plant and increasing the production of light bulbs.[51] Libbey provided Owens a shed near the main factory so he could pursue various projects. Owens continued to work on improving ways of manufacturing lightbulbs. He turned his attention back to developing a mechanical paste-mold bulb machine that used compressed air—instead of a glassblower's lungpower—to make bulbs.[52] His foray into automated glassmaking would lead to a new item: glass tumblers.

In December, 1895, Libbey, Owens, and several other men from Libbey Glass created the Toledo Glass Company, which was formed to profit from Owens' patents. In exchange for rights to his patents for any invention developed during the next

Left: [Fig. 1-30] Libbey cut glass punch bowl wit the Aztec design, circa 1901.

seventeen years, Owens received 800 shares of the new company's stock.[53] They assigned all patents pertaining to new automated glass blowing machines to this new company. A new factory was built with a 14-pot furnace.

With the start of the Toledo Glass Company, Owens turned his attention to the development of machines for automatically blowing glass bottles, as they were in high demand for the growing beer brewing industry and for food packaging. In the next few years Owens, with William Emil Bock and others, worked through the imperfections of the Owens' bottle machine, which revolutionized the glass blowing industry in 1901. The basic design of this machine, with modern updates, is still in commercial use today.

In 1898, the Toledo Glass Company formed the American Lamp Chimney, a company that used a two-part mold that produced a tumbler and chimney in one mold.[54] In 1899, American Lamp Chimney was sold to Macbeth-Evans Glass Company of Pittsburgh, Pennsylvania. Macbeth-Evans, which was the largest producer of lamp chimneys in the country, acquired the rights to Owens's 1895 patent number 534,840 for a glass blowing machine suitable for the production of lamp chimneys.

Top: [Fig. 1-31] Libbey cut glass bowl with the Marcella design.

Right: [Fig. 1-32] Libbey cut glass flower globe with the Corinthian design.

Chapter 2 – The Libbeys and the Community

During the late 1880s, in the midst of establishing his company to Toledo, Libbey met and fell in love with prominent Toledo socialite Florence Scott. Florence was the daughter of Maurice A. Scott and the granddaughter of Jesup W. Scott, who donated the land on which The University of Toledo was built and for whom Scott High School was named.

Florence and Edward were married on June 24, 1890, in her father's house at 2445 Monroe Street, property later gifted to the

Edward D. Libbey

Toledo Museum of Art by the Libbeys. The success of the Libbey Glass Company made the Libbeys prominent and successful members of the Toledo community. They built their home on Scottwood Avenue in Toledo's West End.

Facing page: [Fig. 2-1] The Toledo Museum of Art in 1912. Notice the fountain in the plaza in front of the museum. The Libbeys were key supporters of the museum.

Their love of art and music guided their philanthropic instincts. When presented with the idea of a museum for Toledo, they heartily supported it financially as well as with their time and effort. It was to be a gift to the citizens of Toledo.

The Libbey House

When he first arrived in Toledo, Libbey lived at the Madison Hotel, at 718 Madison Avenue.[55] The newly married couple decided to build their home in Toledo's fashionable West End neighborhood. Just as he did for the Libbey Glass pavilion for the 1893 World's Columbian Exposition, Libbey turned to Toledo architect David L. Stine for the design of their new residence.

Built on a double lot, construction of the shingle and colonial revival style home at 2008 Scottwood Avenue started in 1893 and was completed in 1895.[56] The eighteen room, 10,600 square foot house features a granite stone and wood shingle exterior with a large wraparound veranda, a curved two-story bay, and a full basement with a hidden underground wine cellar.

Throughout the interior of the home, there is elaborate woodwork of cherry, oak, pine, American chestnut, and mahogany. The house boasts five

fireplaces, ten window seats, two built-in safes, fourteen closets, and floor to ceiling Corinthian pillars.

There are three elaborately carved fireplace mantels and Tiffany-style stained glass windows on the grand stairway and curved glass windows on the first floor. The upstairs bathrooms have pedestal sinks, oversized claw tubs, and a marble shower with full body spray plumbing systems.

The dining room features elaborately carved lion heads of which no two are alike. The dining room windows are made of the bottoms of the glass feet of stemware that were hand crafted by Libbey glass factory employees and given as a gift to the Libbeys.

The ceramic tile around the dining room fireplace was hand selected by Florence from a Dutch delft tile company on one of her oversea travels to the Netherlands and each tile is completely different. There is a hidden safe behind the wall next to the fireplace in the dining room. The dining room is made of mahogany and is quite spectacular.

The second floor has a large grand foyer, four bedrooms, two large full baths, and numerous closets. The front smaller bedroom was Florence's sitting room and has a Juliet window that opens to the main stairway and foyer. The third floor was originally designed as servants quarters with five bedrooms, one full bathroom, and a main parlor or central hall area.

Left: [Fig. 2-2] Florence Scott Libbey, around 1906.

Above: [Fig. 2-3] The dining room windows, above, are made of the feet of Libbey Glass stemware and were crafted by Libbey employees and given as a gift to Edward and Florence.

Left: [Fig. 2-4] The Libbey House was named a National Historic Landmark in 1983.

Mrs. Libbey moved out of the house after Edward's death in 1925. Maintained by caretakers Mary and Hattie McConkey, the home sat vacant until Florence's death in 1938. The house remained vacant until 1941, when Dr. Herbert C. Weller bought the home from the Libbey Estate. He sold it in 1965 to the Toledo Society for Crippled Children.

The house was subsequently sold to a private owner in 1980, and served as a single-family residence for nearly three decades, changing hands multiple times until 2008, when it was purchased by the Libbey House Foundation, a non-profit orga-

...spaper in Toledo Receiving the Associated Press News Dispatches

BLADE.

HOME EDITION

OHIO, FRIDAY, NOVEMBER 13, 1925   TWO CENTS   By Carrier, 12 Cents a Week. By Mail Out of City—One Year, $7; Six Months, $4; Three Months, $2.50; One Month, $1.25; One Week, 30c   FOUNDED 1848

AGREES AY U. S. 2,000,000

Provides for l Installments, ning With 000,000.

INTEREST S 2 PER CENT

y Congress and Government pected in hington.

, Nov. 13 (AP)— and Italian debt Saturday will sign for the funding of ebt to the United ted for settlement

---

ART CONNOISSEUR IS STRICKEN
E. D. LIBBEY DIES IN SUITE IN HOTEL SECOR

DEATH CLAIMS E. D. LIBBEY, GLASS KING

Toledo's Foremost Citizen Succumbs to Combined Attack of Pneumonia and Intestinal Influenza.

BURIAL PROBABLY WILL BE IN WOODLAWN CEMETERY

Physicians' Heroic Efforts Defeated by Weakened Heart of Art Connoisseur.

Edward Drummond Libbey, 72, world famous in the glass industry, internationally known art connoisseur and one of Toledo's foremost citizens, died Friday at 9:15 A. M.

Pneumonia was the cause of death. Stricken last Sunday, Mr. Libbey showed little resistance to the disease and died in his suite of rooms, 923 Hotel Secor, despite all that medical talent could nization formed to restore the home to its original grandeur and to preserve the legacy of the Libbey family.

The Foundation purchased the home with the assistance of, in part, Owens-Illinois and several other local glass companies. Today, the primary goal of the Foundation is to make the home available for educational purposes. It also serves as a special events center and hosts occasional historic home tours, the proceeds of which are used to fund its historic preservation and general upkeep.

The home was named a National Historic Landmark in 1983. Situated at the corner of Scottwood and Woodruff Avenues, in the neighborhood now known as The Old West End, it appropriately overlooks the Toledo Museum of Art's new, modern, Glass Pavilion, which opened in 2006.

The Toledo Museum of Art

The idea of an art museum for Toledo was discussed at a Tile Club meeting in late 1900. The Tile Club was a men's organization where members discussed and created art, dined, and socialized.[57] Libbey whole-heartedly supported the idea. His support led to the incorporation of the Toledo Museum of Art on April 18, 1901. The individuals who signed the articles of incorporation were Libbey, Barton Smith, Edmund Osthaus, David L. Stine, Charles Ashley, Robinson Locke, and Almon Whiting. During the museum's first organizational meeting on May 9, 1901, a board of trustees was established with Libbey as its president. Whiting was named museum director. [58]

After its incorporation, the board decided to rent two rooms in the Gardner Building at the corner of Madison Avenue and Superior Street to house its first exhibit. This simple show ran through December of 1901 and was such a success that Libbey felt compelled to secure a permanent home for the museum in 1903.[59] He purchased the former T.P. Brown residence at the corner of Madison Avenue and 13th Street. The museum was at this location until 1908.[60]

Whiting's tenure as museum director was brief, and he was succeeded by George Washington Stevens in 1903. The museum's assets at this time were few, and the collection consisted of a single painting: "Sheep in Pasture" by Willem Steelink, which is still in the museum's collection today.[61]

From the museum's inception, Libbey championed free admission for students and teachers. His idea of a community art museum was unique at the time, and Stevens helped see Libbey's concepts come to fruition. Stevens instituted tours, classes, programs, and lectures for all ages.[62] After a few years, Libbey pushed to drop admission fees for all visitors. Toledoans responded to the idea with enthusiasm, and Toledo soon topped the list of American cities with the highest percentage of its population that visited its local art museum.[63]

In 1906, the Libbeys traveled to Egypt, which was the trendiest tourist destination for wealthy Americans at the time. While abroad, the Libbeys purchased hundreds of artifacts, including two mummies and inner coffins, called cartonnages, which they donated to the museum.[64] These donations led to the museum opening a hugely popular Egyptian gallery. An average of 2,000 visitors a month began to overwhelm the small Madison Avenue building.[65] By 1907 the board began to raise funds for a new building. At this time, Libbey agreed to donate $50,000 towards the new building, with one condition: the Toledo community must raise the same amount by May 1, 1908.[66]

Thousands of children began donating their pocket change to the cause. The community was so committed to the museum that it surpassed Libbey's goal and raised $50,499. The Libbeys, so inspired by the success of the campaign, decided to donate Scott Place – the original Scott homestead on Monroe Street at Scottwood Avenue – to the museum. The mansion was the home of Florence Libbey's recently deceased father, Maurice A. Scott.[67]

Two architects were selected to design the new building: Edward B. Green of Buffalo, New York and Harry W. Wachter of Toledo. Green proposed a Beaux-Arts style façade, but the board had other plans. Stevens contributed a rough sketch of his vision for the museum, which inspired the architects to design a neo-classical building.[68] In white marble and Greek Ionic columns, the façade also featured a frieze of acanthus leaves.[69] The new museum opened on January 17, 1912 to a crowd of eager museum members. Over 1,500 visitors endured the snow and cold to wait in line the following day to view the new exhibitions and see the beautiful new building. The exhibitions were so extraordinary that President William Taft visited the museum a few weeks later.[70] The museum's popularity continued to grow, which led the board to decide that an expansion was necessary again, less than four years later.

In 1916, the museum began to raise funds for an addition. Libbey gave $400,000 to launch the campaign, which the public more then matched with over $600,000 in donations. The expansion project had to be put on hold because of the start of World War I. The post-war economic downturn and high construction costs further delayed the project.[71]

In 1923, Libbey reached out to Edward Green to design an addition to double the size of the existing building. Libbey donated an additional $850,000 to cover the cost of the larger project.[72] Construction began in March 1924, and by the fall of 1925 the museum was readying the space to open. Libbey's sudden death on November 13, 1925, mere weeks before opening, shocked the museum and Toledoans. On January 5, 1926, the museum dedication occurred as planned.[73]

In his will, Libbey created a $1 million endowment fund for the museum. The museum also received his collection of paintings. Less than a year later, the museum was devastated by the death of George Washington Stevens on October 29, 1926. Blake-More Godwin had worked with Stevens and

Libbey since 1916 and succeeded Stevens as director of the museum.[74]

Florence Scott Libbey continued her husband's legacy by donating the lion's share of her fortune to pay for two more additions to the museum, which provided jobs for 2,500 workers during the Great Depression. This included the construction of the Peristyle, the museum's concert hall, which Florence helped design.[75]

Upon her death in 1937, she left the bulk of her estate to the museum. Her legacy and commitment to the arts continues to provide support for the museum today. Because of the Libbey's enduring generosity and commitment to the arts, Godwin purchased many of the museum's most famous pieces, including works by Picasso, Degas, and Van Gogh.[76]

Ojai, California

As notable as Edward Drummond Libbey's contributions were to Toledo, he had a lasting impact on a small town in California.

The town of Nordhoff, California, was a gathering of ramshackle wood framed storefronts with no cohesive style. In the mid-1910s, cities throughout America, including Toledo, were enthusiastically embracing the City Beautiful Movement. While visiting Harry Sinclair, a close friend, Libbey was impressed by the rolling green hills, abundant trout streams, riding trails, and horse farms of the Ojai Valley.

Libbey was enamored by the temperate weather and beautiful scenery, and, in 1909, he hired Pasadena architects Myron Hunt and Elmer Grey to design a craftsman-style bungalow on a large plot of land in Ojai. The home overlooks the Topa Topa mountains and gave him the perfect view of the famous "pink moment" when the setting sun briefly turns the mountains pink.

Libbey decided that transforming the little town into a charming and beautiful retreat was worth his time, effort, and money. After a devastating fire in 1917, the downtown colonnade was rebuilt in the Spanish Colonial Revival style, with Libbey's guidance. The Ojai Inn was torn down, and the land up to the railroad tracks was cleared as an open area for a park. A post office with the tall bell tower anchors the colonnade. The town had been named after Charles Nordhoff, a German journalist who traveled through California and reported on the different cities and towns during his journeys. Because of anti-German sentiment in the World War I era, residents wanted to change the town's name. On January 26, 1917, the Ventura County Supervisor, Tom Clark, said the city would be known as Ojai, derived from the Chumash Indian word for moon. Residents offered to name the town after Libbey, but just as he refused to have the Toledo Museum of Art named after him, he felt Ojai better represented his beloved town.

Another of Libbey's projects was the Arbolada, Spanish for "among the oaks." This was an area of 500 acres of old growth oak trees that Libbey didn't want the railroads to take down. Instead, he

Right: [Fig. 2-6] Main Street in Ojai, California, around 1920.

built three Spanish-styled model homes designed by George Washington Smith, winding roads, and plots of land for both the wealthy and middle class to build their homes and live together in this idyllic setting.

Libbey also wanted to try his hand at ranching, and, in 1923, he hired architect Wallace Neff to design and build stables for cows and horses not far from his bungalow. Soon after Libbey's death in 1925, his wife sold the ranch property and barn to William Lucking Sr., a lawyer for the Ford Motor Company. Lucking hired local designer Austen Pierpont to change the barn into a winter home. Several famous people have called this house their home, including designer Kathryn Ireland and actress Reese Witherspoon.

Walking through Ojai today, Libbey's name is prominently featured in the name of the Libbey Park and the Libbey Bowl, an amphitheater for concerts. Libbey was one of the town's greatest benefactors and residents celebrate his contributions each year during the annual "Ojai Day" outdoor festival. Ojai today is a quiet little town situated in the Ojai Valley of Ventura County, California that has become quite popular with celebrities and movie stars from Los Angeles. The locals are proud it has maintained its quiet and low-key atmosphere, while still having all the charm and culture of much larger towns.

Right: [Fig. 2-7] Edward Libbey on a horse in front of the stables of his ranch in Ojai, California.

Chapter 3 – Innovation and Design

From the 1890s until the late 1910s, the primary product produced at the Libbey factory in Toledo was brilliant cut glass. The 1904 World's Fair in St. Louis was another success for the Libbey Glass Company. It gave the company another chance to display its most impressive pieces of cut glass. The Libbey punchbowl, created for display at the 1904 World's Fair, was touted by *Scientific American* magazine to be the largest piece of cut glass in the world at the time.

A variety of shapes, sizes, and patterns helped establish Libbey Glass as a world leader in brilliant cut glass. However, Libbey knew America's tastes would change with the times and in the late 1890s he directed Owens to spend his time on automation technologies. As it had in the past, this partnership ensured the future success of the Libbey Glass Company.

Facing page: [Fig. 3-1] Workers at the Libbey Glass plant in Toledo, around 1902.

Right: [Fig. 3-2] A plaque made around 1903 by John Rufus "Rufe" Denman and Patrick H. Walker. It features a border cut with the Sultana pattern and the center engraved with the Libbey trade mark.

Above: [Fig. 3-3] The Libbey punchbowl was crafted by Libbey artisan John Rufus "Rufe" Denman for the St. Louis World's Fair in 1904.

Right: [Fig. 3-4] Denman was featured on the cover of the April 30, 1904 edition of Scientific American, cutting and polishing the 25-inch bowl. The magazine described the punch bowl as the "largest piece of cut glass in the world."

SCIENTIFIC AMERICAN

[Entered at the Post Office of New York, N. Y., as Second Class Matter. Copyright, 1904, by Munn & Co.]

Vol. XC.—No. 18.
ESTABLISHED 1845.

NEW YORK, APRIL 30, 1904.

[8 CENTS A COPY
$3.00 A YEAR.

Polishing a 25-Inch Glass Bowl for Exhibition at the St. Louis Exposition. Height with Foot, 24 Inches; Weight of Bowl and Foot Before Cutting, 143 Pounds.

THE LARGEST PIECE OF CUT GLASS IN THE WORLD.—[See page 348.]

Innovation Continues

Having established the Toledo Glass Company in 1895, the Libbey Group formed the Owens Bottle Machine Company on September 3, 1903. After years of research and experimentation, Owens had developed a machine that automated the bottle making process. The purpose of the new company was to build and license the new Owens Bottle Machine. Libbey was president of the new company.

Michael J. Owens

The Owens Bottle Machine, the first commercial bottle making machine, could "suck thick, molten glass from a rotating pot directly into its molds."[77] The new machine could produce more bottles in one hour than a team of glassblowers could produce in a day. It lifted most of its own weight each time it moved a mold to the glass pot, a remarkable feat, considering the 1920 version of the machine consisted of 10,000 parts and weighed 30 tons.[78]

The Owens Bottle Machine Company had to pay the Toledo Glass Company for the use of the rights of the bottle machine. Licensing agreements would soar from five in 1909 to more than 200 in 1920.[79] Around 1903, the company started manufacturing glass bottles on a small scale at a plant in Toledo, but between 1909 and 1920 they had fifteen glass

Above: [Fig. 3-5] Some of the early experiments in automated bottle making. Each bottle is labled with the date and approximate time of the test, along with the names of people present. The bottle second from the left was from an experiment in the early morning hours of December 22, 1899. The experiment was witnessed by M.J. Owens, Thos. Owens, W.E. Bock, and H.C. Wood.

container manufacturing factories located across the United States and was the nation's largest manufacturer of glass bottles.

In 1905, the Toledo Glass Company organized another new company, the Owens European Bottle Machine Company, which built a bottle plant in Trafford Park near Manchester, England, in 1906.[80] Owens-Europe received exclusive rights to the Owens Bottle Machine agreement for Europe and parts of Central and South America. Between 1908 and 1926, 317 Owens Bottle Machine licensing agreements were established on models AC, AD, AE, AL, AN, AQ, and AV. In addition, 119 AR machines were manufactured between 1912 and 1941. The last two original Owens machines in use were AQ models at the Gas City, Indiana, glass container plant of Owens-Illinois, Inc. They were in service until December 17, 1982.

Right: [Fig. 3-6] A pair of Owens Bottle Company trucks, one from Clarksburg, West Virginia, the other from Charleston, West Virginia, in front of the original Toledo factory. The facility, in the 900 block of Wall Street, still stands, but has changed owners over the years and no longer manufactures glass bottles.

Right: [Fig. 3-7] *Michael Owens, third from the left, at a glass factory overseas, overseeing the installation of one of his bottle machines.*

The Owens Bottle Machine not only revolutionized the glass industry, but virtually ended its reliance on child labor. In 1913 the National Child Labor Committee declared the Owens Bottle Machine had done more to eliminate child labor in the glass industry in the U.S. than the organization had through its legislative efforts to date.[81]

In 1905, Libbey Glass developed a new line of glass containers called packer ware. The highly automated production process allowed for mass production of standardized containers. A food processing program began with an idea conceived by the Purity Dairy Company of Windsor, Ontario, Canada to use a basic glass tumbler that could be filled with cottage cheese, washed, and reused as a drinking glass. Within a few years, simple decorations and company logos were added for additional advertising promotions. This product line was extremely profitable for Libbey. They moved quickly to line up additional dairy customers and got closure manufacturers to develop a cap that could be commercially sealed so the tumblers could be reused.

The Owens Bottle machine, with its superior quality and consistency of its finished glass containers, helped lead the government to establish the Pure Food & Drug Act of 1906, thus guaranteeing specific measure of standards for producing these glass containers.[82] This opened the doors for high speed packing and filling lines for various food companies, revolutionizing the food packing industry with such giants as Proctor & Gamble, Heinz, Smuckers, and Kraft Foods

Libbey and Owens' commercial innovation did not stop with the food and beverage industry. Libbey Glass had become an important producer of light bulbs and incandescent lamps. Following the 1893 World's Columbian Exposition in Chicago, Owens also began to experiment with a machine that would automate part of the light bulb manufacturing process. He developed:

> A semi-automatic machine that would blow bulbs into molds. The machine had five rotating arms. Each arm had a device

47

similar to a blow pipe with a mold at the bottom. A glob of molten glass would be picked up onto the pipe, the mold would surround it, and compressed air would blow the glass into the mold. The machine could produce 2,000 bulbs in five hours. While it actually took more workers to produce bulbs using this method, they no longer had to be skilled workers, thus reducing costs.[83]

After the development of the Owens Bottle Machine, the Westlake Machine was the next major machine to be birthed by Owens. It was developed to automate the production of electric light bulbs, yet another exceptional business opportunity. The Westlake Machine was made by the Westlake Machine Company, a business set up by Libbey on Westlake Street in Toledo on November 7, 1907. The new automated blub-blowing machine was ready for production by 1914.

In late 1914, Libbey Glass employee August Kadow was tasked with modifying a version of the Westlake Machine so it could produce tumblers. Like Owens, Kadow was an inventor who had no technical education. While others skilled in engi-

Left: [Fig. 3-8] Cap Lanzinger, one of August Kadow's assistants, next to a partially assembled Westlake Machine.

Facing page: [Fig. 3-9] A completed Westlake Machine producing light bulbs.

WESTLAKE MACHINE

OPERATED ON VACUUM SUCTION FEED PRINCIPLE
HAS 24 BLOWING SPINDLES
PRODUCES 2,400 TO 3,600 PIECES PER HOUR
VALUE EXCEEDS $370,000

49

neering actually did a large part of the work, Kadow was in a position to receive credit and most of the rewards. In 1917 the Kadow Machine went into production. During this time, annealing lehrs – a long, temperature controlled kiln – were developed to handle the large production volume of tumblers. This eventually led to the development of a process of burning off the excess glass or moil at the top of the tumbler to give the tumbler an extremely durable, chip-resistant rim. The Safedge Rim was introduced in 1924 along with a rim chip-age guarantee. Libbey Glass was now able to supply mass produced tumblers to everyday Americans, restau-

Facing page: [Fig. 3-10] A two page ad for Safedge Glassware in the April 5, 1924 edition of the Saturday Evening Post.

Above: [Fig. 3-11] Glasses with a Safedge Rim.

Right: [Fig. 3-12] A worker inspects glasses for defects, right.

rants, hotels and night clubs.

In 1917 another Libbey Glass employee, Edward Danner, helped develop the world's first machine-made glass tubing. At the time, glass tubing was produced by hand. It was a time-consuming process that resulted in tubes with walls of varying thicknesses.[84] The Danner Machine helped revolutionize the production of glass tubing and solid glass rods. In addition to slashing production times, it stabilized production standards and quality, which in turn led to the development of laboratory and scientific products. In 1918 Libbey licensed the use of the Danner Machine to two U.S. companies, General Electric and Kimble Glass Company. On December 12, 1918, Libbey sold its lightbulb making business to General Electric for a sizable profit.

Flat Glass

Born in Fitchburg, Massachusetts in 1861, Irving W. Colburn was an inventor who tried unsuccessfully for years to develop an automated process for the production of continuous flat glass disks.[85] Colburn's idea was to produce flat glass by drawing it out of a furnace in a continuous line or ribbon and then cutting it into pieces. This innovation would make the mass production of window panes possible. He created the Colburn Machine Glass Company in August 1906, but after many failed attempts – he built and tore down fifteen different machines between 1905 and 1912[86] – Colburn was forced to file for bankruptcy.

In 1912 the Toledo Glass Company bought Colburn's patents for making flat glass at a sheriff's auction in Franklin, Pennsylvania, for $15,000. They hired Colburn and put him to work with Owens to perfect the unreliable machine. Over the next four years Toledo Glass invested more than $1 million into the development of a reliable, commercially viable machine. By 1915 the Colburn Machine was able to produce sellable sheets of glass.[87]

Just as the Toledo Glass Company formed a new company once the Owens Bottle Machine was developed, Toledo Glass created another new entity after perfecting the Colburn sheet glass making operations. The Libbey-Owens Sheet Glass company was formed May 18, 1916. The new company bought all the domestic and foreign patent rights from Colburn for the window glass process and began commercial production in a new factory in Charleston, West Virginia on October 17, 1917. The factory was built to produce sheet glass for building materials and eventually automobile windows and windshields.

In the summer of 1898, Edward Ford established the Edward Ford Plate Glass Company on 173 acres of farmland along the Maumee River in Rossford, Ohio. The first case of plate glass was made at the Miami Street plant on October 28, 1899. In 1930, the Libbey-Owens Sheet Glass Company merged with the Edward Ford Glass Company to form the Libbey-Owens-Ford Glass Company.

Libbey-Owens-Ford was one of the world's largest manufacturers of flat glass, providing glass for commercial and architectural building trades as well as windows and windshields for the automotive industry. Libbey-Owens-Ford Glass Company was eventually purchased by Pilkington Glassworks of the United Kingdom, in April of 1986.

Today, the flat glass plant in Rossford is part of the NSG Group, a conglomerate based in Tokyo with annual revenues of $7 billion. The Rossford plant has two production lines that run 24 hours a day, 365 days a year. Barring any unforeseen issues, the machines are only shut down completely every fifteen to eighteen years.[88]

Left: [Fig. 3-13] The Libbey-Owens-Ford plant in Rossford, Ohio, around 1965.

Above: [Fig. 3-14] An assortment of wine glasses made around 1903 by Libbey Glass.

Right: [Fig. 3-15] A vase of colorless glass overlaid with ruby glass made between 1910 and 1915 by Libbey Glass.

Facing page: [Fig. 3-16] A bowl of colorless glass overlaid with deep blue glass made between 1920 and 1925 by Libbey Glass.

"The New Era in Glass" and Owens-Illinois

In 1917, with cut glass sales on the downturn, Libbey Glass turned back to a hand-made, colored glass process and re-introduced the Amberina Collection, a two-toned glass product using amber and ruby glass. This sold modestly and was eventually discontinued, primarily due to the lack of skilled craftsmen.

When Edward Drummond Libbey arrived in Toledo in 1888, he had $100,000 in assets. By the time Libbey stepped down as president of Libbey Glass in 1920, his net worth was $40 million. His principle associates at the time were Owens, Clarence Brown, Frederick L. Geddes, and William S. Walbridge. Libbey remained chairman of the board until his death in 1925. Jefferson D. Robinson, Sr. was named president of Libbey Glass in 1920. Upon

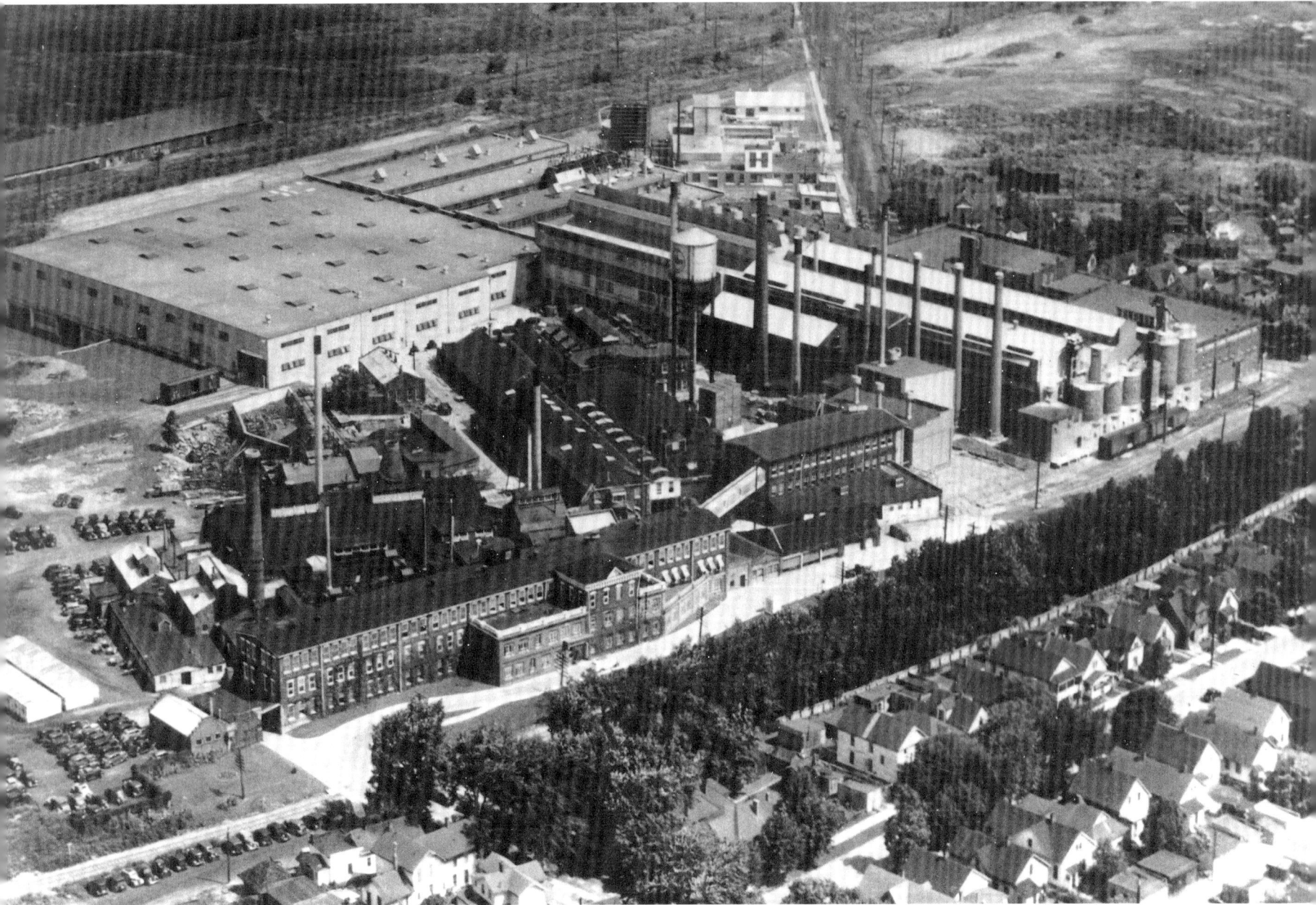

his death in 1929, he was succeeded by his eldest son, Joseph W. Robinson.

In the 1930s, the Libbey Glass Company ventured into more contemporary styles with the Nash Series and then the Modern American Series, although none of these styles proved to be as successful as Libbey's brilliant cut glass. Sales of cut glass began declining due to imports and cut glass starting to slip out of fashion. In 1931, Libbey Glass hired chief designer Arthur Douglas Nash from the defunct Tiffany Glass factory in Corona, New York, to create and design a new line of superior quality glassware that would be called "The New Era in Glass." Libbey Glass president Joseph W. Robinson gave Nash complete backing for this collection. Many thought the new pieces lacked originality, but all agreed they showed outstanding craftsmanship. The fabulous new Libbey-Nash series of over 80 patterns – many of which never went to production and were only sampled – was formally introduced in 1933 with extravagant showrooms and press reviews.

The work was "noted for its beauty of form and was intricately decorated with cutting, engraving, and such surface effects as overlay, threading, and

Facing page: [Fig. 3-17] The Libbey Glass factory in Toledo, around 1930.

Right: [Fig. 3-18] A chalice of colorless and red blown and engraved glass with the Druid pattern, designed by Arthur Douglas Nash around 1933.

A pair of designs by Arthur Douglas Nash. Left: [Fig. 3-19] A cranberry colored goblet with a Bristol pattern. Below: [Fig. 3-20] A pair of champagne glasses.

colored accents."[89] Advertisements at the time boasted "no machine in the world can produce the same graceful lines, the same flashing brilliance, that identify the handiwork of the master glass craftsman." Stemware prices ranged from $10 to $2,500 a dozen. Unfortunately, this new luxury line of glass was out-priced for the status of the nation's depressed economy and lasted only one year.

Facing page: [Fig. 3-21] The showroom of J.J. Freeman Jewelers, 626 Jefferson Avenue, Toledo, around 1930. Notice the sign proclaiming "Libbey Cut Glass, The World's Best" on the back wall.

Also in the 1930s, Libbey Glass developed the first machine to decorate glass tumblers. This opened the doors to countless new retail opportunities that would continue to help establish the Libbey name in every American household. The first decorating machines were limited in the complexity of design and colors. Over time, they became much more automated and could achieve a number of different applied colors. Some of the early decorated tumblers were quite simple in design but still

A trio of glasses, all designed by Arthur Douglas Nash around 1933. Facing page, left: [Fig. 3-23] A colorless and opalescent pink glass chalice with the Victoria pattern. Facing page, center: [Fig. 3-24] A colorless and green glass chalice. Facing page, right: [Fig. 3-25] A colorless and blue glass chalice with the Stourbridge pattern.

Below: [Fig. 3-22] A free blown clear glass punch bowl with applied lily pad prunts, designed by Arthur Douglas Nash between 1931 and 1935.

very collectible. Despite the success of this new machine, the Great Depression had a deleterious impact on the financial footing of Libbey Glass. The company was also struggling under the burden of having heavily invested in Nash's new lines, which, despite being highly sought after now, did not generate anywhere near the anticipated sales.

Owens-Illinois (O-I) was formed on April 17, 1929, by the merger of the Owens Bottle Glass Company (1911-1929) and the Illinois Glass Company (1873-1929). In 1935 O-I purchased the Libbey Glass Company for $5 million, with John H. Wright succeeding Joseph W. Robinson as president of Libbey Glass. Libbey remained a wholly-owned subsidiary of Owens-Illinois for a few years before it was made an operating division in 1938.

Libbey's packer ware program was one of the reasons O-I was interested in the assets of Libbey Glass. In 1937, Libbey's tie-in with Walt Disney's wildly popular movie "*Snow White and the Seven Dwarfs*" proved to be a highly successful association. Walt Disney himself visited the Toledo plant to discuss the idea of decorating small glass tumblers with images of Snow White and the Seven Dwarfs to help promote his new movie.

This was the start of a new phenomenon in glassware, known as premium giveaways or promotions. Filling tumblers with cottage cheese or processed cheese proved to be a highly successful promotional idea. Yearly production of decorated tumblers during that time period reached into the millions.

With the success of the packer ware product line and profits at an all time high, the O-I management team decided Libbey should once again be a leader in the fine glass arena. This was not so much a decision to dominate the glassware gift market, but a means to sell other Libbey glassware. Harold Boeschenstein and John Wright hand-picked Edwin W. Fuerst to design a new line of crystal products called Modern American.

Fuerst, a former student at the Toledo Museum of Art and head of the Package Department at O-I,[90] understood the basic design principles of glass. He, along with a few of Libbey's most skilled craftsmen, was able to create an extraordinary collection worthy of the name Modern American. Developed

Edwin W. Fuerst

in 1939, the new glass composition was called "new crystal" because its color was equal to that of any glass in the world. It was introduced in 1940 at the Crystal Room in New York's Gotham Hotel and the Modern American line was soon featured in 300 stores across the country.

During World War II, Libbey's craftsmen were needed to make radar, x-ray, and electronic tubes and other war-time materials instead of household glassware. After the war, Libbey's management faced the necessary challenges of either rebuilding

Left: [Fig. 3-26] Libbey craftsman John Rufus "Rufe" Denman works on a piece from the Modern American series.

63

Left: [Fig. 3-27] Embassy Pattern cocktail glasses designed by Edwin W. Fuerst around 1939.

Below: [Fig. 3-28] An Old Fashioned glass with Knickerbocker pattern designed around 1932.

Facing page: [Fig. 3-29] An automated glass machine.

the original 1888 hand shop factory or closing it down. The decision to close the hand shop was difficult and meant the Modern American series was the last hand-made glass ever made by Libbey.

Post War and Freda Diamond

With the war over, Libbey emerged as America's oldest and largest glassmaker, supplying glass tumblers and stemware to almost every major retailer and foodservice establishment in the country. Decorated glassware by Libbey could be found in almost every American home. Having discontinued the production of hand-made cut crystal as well as all of the contemporary hand-made glass series, Libbey now concentrated on the automatic high-volume techniques and production that would help the company become America's most recognized brand in glassware.

In late 1947, Owens-Illinois purchased the outstanding stock of Sharpe, Inc. of Buffalo, New York. Sharpe was founded in 1914 and had purchased, cut, and polished many Libbey blanks into cut glass pieces for various retail use. Sharpe became a wholly-owned subsidiary of the Libbey Glass Division. The Sharpe Company was liquidated from Libbey and Owens-Illinois in 1950.

In 1948, Libbey developed the first fully automatic machine to manufacture stemware. The new stemware lines were instant successes with bars and restaurants nationwide. This would help establish Libbey as a premier leader in the foodservice industry.

Libbey sales nearly doubled during the first six years under Owens-Illinois. In 1942, Libbey's marketing department began planning for postwar projects. That same year, Libbey hired Freda Diamond (whose married name was Freda Baruch), a leading design consultant from New York City. Diamond was hired to help Libbey with marketing and product development. She made coast-to-coast

trips to survey the market of household glassware. Her relationship with Libbey lasted nearly 40 years and also included design work. One of Diamond's first proposals, Hostess Sets, was promoted through lively advertisements in national magazines. Hostess Sets were packaged sets of drinking glasses decorated with playful pictures. It proved to be a very successful concept for Libbey.

Over the years, Diamond was behind every design that Libbey produced. She was instrumental in product development early on with managers John Harbaugh and Lou Alesi; New Product Development Director, Jerry "Obie" Obendorfer; Libbey General Manager, Curly Achenbach; and Design Director, John Tuttle. During the 1950s, several of Diamond's glassware lines earned the prestigious "Good Design" award from the Museum of Modern Art in New York City. She was named the "Designer for Everybody" by *Life* magazine in 1954. Among her most famous and successful designs was a decorated glass pattern called Gold and Silver Foliage (1956) along with Harvest Wheat, Gold Coins, Mediterranean, and Safari. Her classic design and her Apollo design were both recognized with a design award from the Museum of Modern Art in New York City.

Top: [Fig. 3-30] An early hostess set featuring one of Freda Diamond's foliage designs.

Left: [Fig. 3-31] Diamond created the initial artwork on layers of acetate.

Facing page: [Fig. 3-32] A decorating machine.

On November 2, 1959, Libbey Glass, with approval from parent Owens-Illinois, purchased the Keystone Brass Works of Erie, Pennsylvania, a highly automated producer of melamine plastic dinnerware. Libbey sold off the brass division and changed the name of the company to Applied Plastics Company and eventually to Libbey Plastics, Inc. When Libbey discovered it could not make and sell melamine products profitably, it liquidated the company on October 1, 1962.

In 1960 and the years that followed, decorated tumbler sets with Diamond's designs were successful and profitable. New techniques and processes were developed to continue the decorated tumbler business. Diamond believed design for the upscale retail market helped to influence design in the everyday market as well. She pushed Libbey to new heights in design and product development until her retirement in the late 1980s.

Diamond and her husband, industrial designer

Right: [Fig. 3-33] Freda Diamond, first on the left, at the opening night of "A Tradition of 150 Years," an exhibit at the Toledo Museum of Art in 1963. Also pictured are, from left, Jamie DeLong, Ted Harbaugh, and Carl Fauster.

Alfred Baruch, had their offices and design studio in their brownstone at 140 East 37th Street, in the Murray Hill section of Manhattan, New York. Diamond traveled numerous times to China and Asia in the 1930s and 1940s. She donated the bulk of her papers and designs to the National Museum of American History's Division of Ceramic and Glass in 1997. Diamond died in 1998.

Between improvements in production, efficiencies at the factory, new designs, and aggressive marketing campaigns, from 1943 to 1968 Libbey's annual sales increased from $7 million to $40 million.[91]

Right: [Fig. 3-34] Glass with the Nob Hill pattern, designed by Freda Diamond about 1963.

Above: [Fig. 3-35] Citation, designed by Freda Diamond about 1966, was one of Libbey's most popular designs for ore than 40 years.

Derby glasses, from left to right. [Fig. 3-36] 1986, [Fig. 3-37] 1940, [Fig. 3-38] 1968, and [Fig. 3-39] 1975.

Libbey Glass and the Kentucky Derby

Established in 1875, the Kentucky Derby has been called the "Fastest Two Minutes in Sports." It is the first race of the American Triple Crown, which includes the Preakness Stakes and the Belmont Stakes.

After the 1938 Kentucky Derby, the Churchill Downs staff realized they were consistently running short of water glasses because fans were taking them as souvenirs to commemorate the race day. Churchill Downs contacted Harry M. Stevens, a suc-

cessful sports concession catering businessman, to develop a souvenir glass to serve the now famous mint julep derby cocktail.

In 1939, he designed a decorated, dated glass to commemorate that year's race. Sales of the glasses soared. In the early years, about 100,000 commemorative glasses were produced each year. Today production exceeds 700,000 glasses a year. Every year the glasses were produced with a different design and colors, but they always included a list of every derby winner.

Libbey started producing the Derby Glass Collection in the early 1940s and continued to do so until the mid 2010s. Charles Rice III was the special markets manager at Libbey and for many years oversaw the development of almost every derby glass produced. His unique sales style solidified Libbey's hold on the Kentucky Derby business for over 75 years.

Today, there are hundreds, even thousands, of derby glass collectors. A few of the original derby glasses from the early 1940s, especially the ones from 1941 to 1944, have been known to sell for over $17,000 per glass.

Chapter 4 – Acquisitions and Independence

With long-range projections showing western states would account for at least one-third of future Libbey glassware sales, in 1961 the Libbey Glass Division of Owens-Illinois built the first new glass factory west of the Mississippi River near Los Angeles. According to Owens-Illinois chairman Raymon Mulford, the company wanted to build in Los Angeles county, in part, because of "attractive gas fuel and good transportation facilities, and excellent sources of such essential items as sand,"[92] some of the same traits that lured Edward Libbey to Toledo in the 1880s.

The 318,000 square foot factory was built on an 89-acre site near the intersection of Valley Boulevard and Brea Canyon Road in City of Industry, California.[93] Dedicated on September 28, 1962, the factory originally had two 150-ton furnaces, five glass blowing machines, and more than 375 employees. It was capable of producing 100 million glasses a year.

It manufactured blown tumblers and one-piece and two-piece stemware. At the plant's dedication,

Mulford told the *Los Angeles Times* the company was "channeling every dollar it [could] mobilize into growth."[94]

Louisiana and Pennsylvania

In 1973, eleven years after dedicating its new facility in City of Industry, Owens-Illinois purchased the former Libbey-Owens-Ford sheet glass plant in Shreveport, Louisiana for $1.2 million. First opened in 1922, LOF shuttered the plant in late 1971, citing

Facing page: [Fig. 4-1] The Libbey plant in Toledo, around 1974.

Right: [Fig. 4-2] The Libbey plant in City of Industry, California.

loss of market share in the bulk window glass market due to competition from foreign producers.[95]

With the installation of the "A" furnace in 1973, Shreveport's Jewella Road facility was converted to produce Libbey glass products, focusing on tumblers and pressed glassware. Bob Falter was named plant manager. The newly converted glass factory was in full operation by early 1974, enabling Libbey to produce pressed tumblers at a greater rate, reducing production costs. With 600 employees, the Shreveport plant has over 691,000 square feet of manufacturing and distribution space. The entire facility covers 54 acres and includes a warehouse, distribution center, and an outlet store.

As production rates increased, new shape designs followed. One of Libbey's most famous and most heavily copied designs – the Gibraltar pressed tumbler and stemware line – was designed by Freda Diamond in 1977. Inspired by a beautiful Baccarat cut crystal collection Diamond saw on one of her many trips to Europe, it is one of the most successful glass tumbler collections in Libbey's history.

In 1968 Owens-Illinois named Curly Achenbach general manager of the Libbey Glass Division. Other key Libbey Glass directors included Jerry "Obie" Obendorfer, director, New Product Development; John Tuttle, director of design; Bob Wacke, marketing director; and Diamond, design consultant. As a result of the efforts of Achenbach's team, in 1975 Libbey introduced a new series of blown jars, bean pots, bubble balls, hanging terrariums, vases, and canisters called Glass Creations. The success of the Glass Creations line helped establish Libbey as a front runner in the world-wide retail glassware market.

Owens-Illinois was not done growing its Libbey Glass Division. In 1975, it turned its attention to Pennsylvania, another state with a rich history of glass production.

The L.E. Smith Glass Company was established in 1907 when Charles Wible and Lewis E. Smith acquired an Anchor Hocking glass factory in Jeannette, Pennsylvania. Initial plans called for the new business to produce jars for Smith's gourmet mustard. After Smith left the business, Wible continued to run the factory under the L.E. Smith name.[96] The company produced some of the first headlight lenses for Henry Ford's Model T, and began manufacturing colored tabletop giftware around 1920.

The company produced covered candy dishes, glass baskets, vases, and footed bowls. One of its most famous pressed patterns was called Moon & Stars. The glassware was available in an array of colors, including cobalt blue, amethyst, yellow, amber, green, and pink. L.E. Smith, however, gained notoriety as the only glass manufacturer at the time that could produce black glass. L.E. Smith Glass was a leader in vintage or depression-styled colored pressed glass giftware through most of the 1970s and 1980s.

The Libbey Glass Division of Owens-Illinois purchased L.E. Smith Glass Company, which was then based in Mt. Pleasant, Pennsylvania, on December 8, 1975 and ran it as a separate company. Libbey subsequently sold the L.E. Smith operation on

December 31, 1986. One of the last glass factories in the region, the factory struggled over the next 19 years until it finally closed in 2005.

Libbey-St. Clair

While Toledo was the Glass Capital of the World, other cities also laid claim to their role in the world's glass industry. Located about 100 miles northeast of Toledo, Wallaceburg, Ontario was Canada's "Glasstown." The glass industry came to Wallaceburg in 1895 when the Sydenham Glass Company opened on the banks of the Sydenham River. In 1913 it became the Dominion Glass Company, which evolved into Domglas Ltd. in 1976.

In 1978, Domglas and Libbey formed a new entity, Libbey-St. Clair Inc., with ownership split evenly between Domglas and Owens-Illinois. Philip N. Jacobs, general manager of the St. Clair Division of Domglas was named the new firm's first president. Initial plans called for the Wallaceburg factory to transition from making containers, such as baby food jars and liquor bottles to glass tableware.[97]

Libbey-St.Clair went on to produce a variety of glass products. Initially known for producing glass

Left: [Fig. 4-3] The batch tower at Libbey-St. Clair in Wallaceburg, Ontario. The tower stored and mixed ingredients for glass, including crushed limestone, recycled glass from the factory, sand from Rockwell, Michigan, and soda ash from Amherstburg, Ontario.

Left: [Fig. 4-4] Gibraltar glass and tumblers. Designed by Freda Diamond in 1977, Gibraltar is one of the most copied designs in Libbey history.

Below: [Fig. 4-5] Deco Bottles made at the Wallaceburg, Ontario plant.

insulator parts and packer ware products, the firm developed a complete line of tabletop products including pressed ware, individual station bottles, one-piece stemware, tumblers, and decorated glassware. The Toledo new product development team visited Libbey-St. Clair many times in the early 1980s to work on various new products for both the Canadian and United States markets.

One of the most successful product lines manufactured by Libbey-St. Clair was the individual station product line "Deco Bottles," which was spearheaded by Paul Baughman, then retail marketing director. The new line was a collection of wine and

vinegar bottles, canisters with cork tops and wire bale clip tops, and various jars and containers, all produced in Spanish green glass color.

Achenbach and his design team helped turn Libbey Glass into a profitable division for Owens-Illinois. When he retired from the Libbey Division in 1985, Aschenbach was hired by O-I to run their Ravenhead Tableware Division in England.

Lou Alesi took over as general manager of Libbey for a few years, followed by Terry Wilkinson and then by John Meier. Meier started with Libbey in 1970 along with Richard Reynolds and Dutch Ashton. He ran the Durobar Division of Owens-Illinois in Belgium for a few years before returning to Toledo as marketing and sales manager.

Libbey and Owens-Illinois Part Ways

Owens-Illinois was purchased in 1987 by Kohlberg, Kravis, Roberts & Company, a New York-based investment firm, in a $3.66 billion leveraged buyout. In 1993, in an effort to reduce its debt, O-I announced plans to sell off its Libbey Glass operations for an estimated $225 million. The sale of the Libbey operation signaled O-I's plans to focus on its glass and plastic packaging business. At the time, Libbey was the leading producer of glass tableware in the United States and one of the largest glass tableware manufacturers in the world. The company had sales of $279 million in 1992.[98]

After 58 years as a subsidiary to a company that could trace its own roots back to the original Libbey Glass Company, on June 18, 1993, Libbey Inc.

Left: [Fig. 4-6] Robert Zollweg and Freda Diamond in 1994.

became an independent company once more. The initial public offering, started in November of 1992, was spearheaded by Meier and Reynolds, along with legal and financial assistance from Art Smith, Diane Bowland, Ken Boerger, and others. The new company's Board of Directors included Meier, Reynolds, Joe Lemieux, and Terry Wilkinson. Peter Howell and Bill Foley were added later that year.

Meier was named chairman and CEO; Reynolds, CFO; Ken Wilkes, treasurer; Art Smith, secretary and legal counsel; Bob Falter, vice president Manufacturing; and George Templin, vice president Human Resources. In 1995, Dutch Ashton was named Vice President of Foodservice Sales; Dan Ibele, Director of Marketing and Sales; Tim Paige, Human Resources; and Ken Boerger, Finance.

When Libbey went public in 1993, it moved the company's headquarters to the Ohio Building on Madison Avenue in downtown Toledo. Since

1982, Libbey's corporate office had been in Toledo's newest skyscraper, the Owens-Illinois building at One SeaGate, on the banks of the Maumee River in downtown Toledo. Libbey Inc. eventually moved its headquarters from the Ohio Building to the Edison Building at 300 Madison Avenue, where the company is still located to this day.

Following the IPO, Libbey had manufacturing facilities in City of Industry, California; Shreveport, Louisiana; and Toledo, Ohio. Libbey Inc. also purchased the remaining 50 percent of the Wal-laceburg, Ontario Libbey-St. Clair plant, making it the sole owner. In the ensuing years, more would come, and some would go.

A newly independent company with new leadership, new goals for growth, and new product development initiatives, Libbey explored new trends in the retail and foodservice channels. The company needed to grow in other ways besides new glass products. As part of that growth, Libbey Inc. made its first major acquisition: the purchase of Syracuse China of Syracuse, New York, in 1995.

Syracuse China and Vitro-Crisa

Founded in 1871 in Geddes, New York as the Onondaga Pottery Company, the business initially produced only earthenware. In the late 1880s, the company developed a translucent chinaware that it called Syracuse China, using the name of the nearby, larger town of Syracuse, New York. The first American-made vitreous china, it won the High Award Medal at the 1893 World's Columbian Exposition in Chicago.

The company moved to a new factory at 2801 Court Street, in nearby Lyncourt, New York in 1921. The new facility was built to handle the growing demand for the company's fine residential china and commercial hotel and restaurant ware. The company's Shadowtone design helped it weather the Great Depression of the 1930s. During World War II, the company produced millions of pieces of china for both military and civilian use. Aside from bowls, plates, and mugs, the plant also helped develop and manufacture a non-metallic anti-tank landmine for the war that could work in any soil and under water.

Following the end of the war, production turned

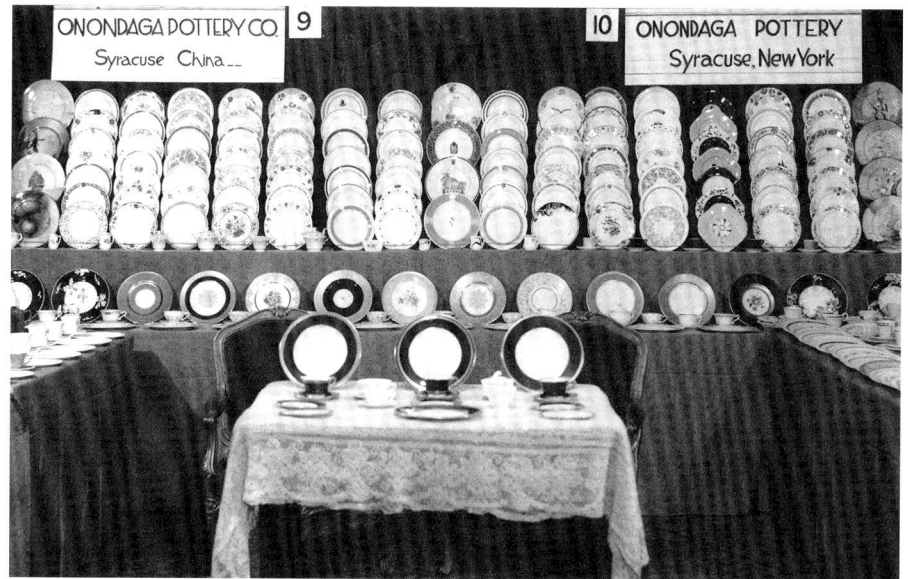

Top: [Fig. 4-8] An Onondaga Pottery Company display of Syracuse China at a trade show in 1938.

Right: [Fig. 4-9] Onondaga Pottery workers assemble M-5 ceramic anti-tank mines in 1943.

Facing page: [Fig. 4-7] Workers outside of the Onondaga Pottery Company in 1871.

Above: [Fig. 4-10] Designed in the late 1990s, Cantina dinnerware was the first solid colored glazed dinnerware produced at the Syracuse plant.

back to commercial chinaware, and generations of workers from the Syracuse, New York, area relied on the plant for employment. In 1966 the company formally changed its name to Syracuse China. Following a change in ownership in 1971, the business became Syracuse China Corporation.

In 1978 Syracuse China Corp. merged with Canadian Pacific Investments, Ltd. As a subsidiary of CPI, Syracuse acquired two Pennsylvania companies: Mayer China Company in 1984 and Shenango Pottery in 1988. Syracuse closed both facilities and consolidated all of the product lines at the Syracuse plant. In 1989, Canadian Pacific decided to sell Syracuse. Pfaltzgraff Company, of York, Pennsylvania, was the successful bidder, and became the new owner of the Syracuse China Company.

When Libbey Inc. purchased Syracuse from Pfaltzgraff in 1995, Chuck Goodman was the president and general manager. The new owners had to learn about American made ceramic dinnerware and how to further automate the plant to meet the demands of the food service dinnerware market. Libbey added "Cantina," a colored glaze dinnerware collection designed by Libbey's Creative Director, Robert Zollweg, and numerous oversized entree bowls.

The 1990s were great years for colored glassware. Libbey continued to introduce colored glassware for the retail channel, including new colors such as peach, Spanish green, misty blue, Mediterranean and cobalt blue, tawny, and smoke.

Colored glassware was difficult to produce. It was not easy for manufacturing to get in and out of color, but demand was high and manufacturing made it happen. Colored glassware lasted for another dozen years before it became too difficult to justify the additional manufacturing costs. Today, Libbey still produces some colored glassware, mainly Spanish green, cobalt blue, tawny or mocha, and smoke grey.

After purchasing Syracuse China, Libbey looked to continue to grow in the retail arena. Two years later, in 1997, Libbey entered into a joint venture with Vitro-Crisa of Monterrey, Mexico. Libbey agreed to buy 49 percent of Crisa and its entire World Tableware Division (WTI). This had a profound impact on Libbey's product assortment in both retail and foodservice sectors. Crisa gave Libbey low cost retail product and WTI gave them entry level ceramic dinnerware and flatware for the foodservice markets.

Libbey now had a complete tabletop assortment available in all channels of marketing. Libbey also developed a complete line of stainless steel flatware and ceramic dinnerware under the Libbey brand for the retail market. Spearheaded by Karen Young, Libbey's Retail Marketing Manager, and Zollweg, it was introduced at the International Housewares Show in Chicago in March of 1998 with mixed reviews and was discontinued in 2000.

The people and culture of Crisa were a natural fit for the two companies to work together and develop profitable product for all markets. One of the most significant products Crisa has produced is a glass tumbler line called "Impressions." Over time, it has become the number one selling tumbler line

Above: [Fig. 4-11] Impressions, the top selling glass design in the North American retail market for Libbey. Produced at the Monterrey plant.

in the United States and Canada.

While Libbey Inc. was expanding its product line up and acquiring new factories, management made the difficult decision to close its Wallaceburg, Ontario facility in 1999. According to Libbey vice president Arthur Smith, while the plant was profitable, increases in production efficiency had not

Left: [Fig. 4-12] Winchester was designed by Freda Diamond in the 1980s. A durable pressed glass piece, it still maintains strong sales.

Below left: [Fig. 4-13] Designed by Freda Diamond, Chivalry was a very popular Libbey design in the 1970s and 1980s.

Below Right: [Fig. 4-14] Designed in 1949 as a mixing glass, the 5139 Pub Glass is one of Libbey's most popular designs and is still in production today at the the Shreveport plant.

been met with an equivalent increase in demand. The Wallaceburg plant, referred to by locals as "The Glass," was selected for closure because of its proximity to the Toledo factory and because it was the only Libbey plant that produced bottleware, a product Libbey was going to discontinue.[99] The plant's closure on May 31, 1999 idled 560 workers.

Below: [Fig. 4-15] Vina is one of the strongest performing stemware collections in the company's history, even surpassing Freda Diamond's wildly popular Citation design from the 1960s. Vina is produced at the Toledo plant.

Chapter 5 – Design and the Modern Era

The New Year's Eve celebration of 2000 was huge, especially for the foodservice industry. Celebrating the New Year at restaurants and at home was big. Sales were at an all time high and business was good for Libbey Inc.

The management team began their exploration in acquisitions, and over the next eight years, Libbey acquired several different companies to round out its tabletop product offerings, even venturing in the back of the house (a foodservice term for equipment used in the kitchen versus a product used in the bar or dining room part of a restaurant), which was a first for Libbey.

A European Presence

In 2002, Libbey purchased Royal Leerdam, a major manufacturer of high quality glass stemware and popular wine glasses from BSN Glasspack for 42.3 million euros. Based in Leerdam, Netherlands, a city 30 miles southeast of Amsterdam, the company was founded in 1878. Named NV Nederland-

Facing page: [Fig. 5-1] Made at the Toledo factory, Stemless was designed in 2004 and is a consistent strong seller.

sche Glasfabriek Leerdam in 1891, in 1915 the company hired a team of designers who were charged with making "an aesthetically-pleasing" assortment of products for the consumer market.

In 1938, the company merged with NV Vereenigde Glasfabrieken, and focused production efforts on household and consumer glassware. On the occasion of the company's 75th anniversary in 1953, the glass factory was granted permission to call itself royal, and the international brand name Royal Leerdam was introduced. Five years later, the company's first mechanically produced glass series was launched.

Over the coming decades, Royal Leerdam continued to innovate, and released noteworthy designs such as Bouquet in 1983. Designed by Floris Meydam, it was the wineglass with the highest stem and largest bowl on the market. In 2000, Royal Leerdam unveiled a new glassware range, Allure, which featured longer horizontal designs and an extremely long and thin stem.

Leerdam's design team, lead by Siem van der Marel, created a collection of stemware and beautiful hand blown art glass under the name of Royal Leerdam Crystal. Leerdam Crystal was the design part of the traditional glass factory in Leerdam. Libbey sold the Leerdam Crystal portion of the company to Royal Delft in 2007. Royal Delft is the leading producer of authentic Delftware (Delft Blue) and special ceramic products in small quantities.

Also in 2002, Libbey purchased its first back of the house manufacturing company, Traex. A plastic manufacturing company based in Dane, Wisconsin, Traex was founded in a rented hanger at the Madison, Wisconsin airport in 1977. It made plastic trays for fast food companies, and was purchased in 1985 by Menasha Corp. Two years later, Traex purchased the assets of Dipcut Inc., and became a producer of glass syrup pitchers, condiment squeeze bottles, and salt and pepper shakers. By the time Libbey purchased Traex, the company was

also making Rack Max dishwasher racks and service trays for schools and wait staff. Seven years later, in 2011, Libbey sold its Traex operations to Vollrath Corporation, of Sheboygan, Wisconsin.

In 2004, more than 40 years after it opened, Libbey officials announced the City of Industry plant outside of Los Angeles, would close in early 2005, idling 200 workers. At the time, it manufactured drinking glasses and was one of five Libbey plants in the United States. According to then-Libbey chairman and CEO John Meier, the decision to close the plant was due to "increasing demands from customers and growing international competitive pressures," which required the company to reduce costs and improve profit margins.[100]

As part of its continuing effort to become a world-wide supplier of high-quality, machine-produced glass tableware, in early 2005 Libbey purchased another glass manufacturing company,

Below: [Fig. 5-2] Designed by Robert Zollweg, this reinterpretation of the classic hobstar pattern from the late 1800s was introduced in 2000, and was sold by Macy's and other national retailers.

Crisal, from Vista Alegre Atlantis SGPS, SA, for 28 million euro. Based in Marina Grande, Portugal, about 70 miles north of Lisbon, Crisal produced and marketed blown and pressed tumblers, stemware, and glassware accessories. The majority of its sales were in Portugal and Spain. The Crisal division eventually merged with Royal Leerdam to become Libbey Europe. Libbey was now a world leader in glass tabletop products for the retail, business to business, and foodservice markets.

[Fig. 5-3 and Fig. 5-4] Made at Libbey's factory in Portugal, the new hobstar tumbler is the company's top selling glass in Europe.

Expanding in Mexico and to China

In 2006, Libbey purchased the remaining 51 percent of Crisa from Vitro-Crisa in Monterrey, Mexico, giving Libbey 100 percent ownership of Crisa. This would eventually become known as Libbey Mexico, but it is still referred to it as Crisa.

Crisa was founded in 1938 in Monterrey, Mexico, as part of Vidriera Monterrey, now known as Vitro and then Vitro-Crisa. The initial factory, Plant C, opened in 1938 and had 200 workers. Over the years Crisa grew, adding a second plant in 1940. In 1942 the company built its first continuous oven,

Facing page and this page: [Fig. 5-5, Fig. 5-6, and Fig. 5-7] Designed by Royal Leerdam and made in Portugal, this design is known as Caret. It is sold in the United States as Montclair.

and added two more over the next six years. In 1956, Crisa acquired Cristales Mexicanos, SA, a manufacturer of tableware and household products, including the company's plant in Monterrey, Mexico.

Design and innovation continued in the coming years, with Crisa developing different brands of glass and crystal. In 1962, the firm introduced Pyr-O-Rey, a popular line of tableware, ovenware, and other kitchenware, known for its ability to withstand extreme temperatures.

Two years later, Crisa built its first atomizing machine, allowing the company to apply various colors to tableware. Luster Shell, as it became known, was popular in Middle East markets. In 1975, Crisa opened plant K2 to manufacture its lead crystal brand of products known as Kristaluxus. Crisa had a brief strategic alliance with Corning Inc. from 1992 to 1994, prior to Libbey's initial acquisition of 49 percent of Crisa in 1997.

Along with its press and blown production machines, Crisa has a state-of-the-art hand shop that is able to produce hand-made looking pitchers, vases, and other home decor products sold worldwide. The hand shop is unique to the worldwide glass manufacturing processes because most are highly automated.

Crisa has over 2,800 employees on a 28.6 acre manufacturing campus, with over 75 acres and numerous factory and warehouse buildings in Monterrey, Nuevo Leon, Mexico. It also has seventeen outlet stores throughout Mexico.

Having acquired a pair of well-established European glassmakers and solidifying its hold on North American production, Libbey turned its attention to the east, and established the Libbey Glassware China Company, Ltd. In 2007, Libbey announced plans to build an entirely new tableware glass manufacturing plant in Langfang, China, about 50 miles east of Beijing. The $52 million state-of-the-art tableware glass plant would manufacture high-quality glasses for wine, beer, milk, juices, soft drinks and other beverages, as well as ashtrays, candleholders, and other glassware. The engineering, construction, and 2007 start up was headed by Terry Hartman and Wayne Zitkus, along with engineers from Toledo, Leerdam, and recent Libbey retirees.

Its primary manufacturing purpose is to produce glassware for the Chinese market, not to import it to the United States. Libbey China produces and manufactures pressed and blown product that have been previously developed in the United States. They are currently starting to design their

Facing page:
[Fig. 5-8] The Yucatan pitcher was designed by Robert Zollweg in 2016 and is handmade at Libbey's plant in Monterrey.

Right: [Fig. 5-9] Selene Serveware was designed in 2009 by Robert Zollweg and is made at the Monterrey plant.

own new product for the Chinese retail and food-service markets. Libbey-China sits on 50 acres, has over 450,000 square feet of manufacturing and warehouse space, and 400 employees. In 2018, Libbey China became part of Libbey Europe.

Art, Design, and Premium Products

Based at the Toledo plant, the art department was responsible for developing the artwork for all decorated glassware produced at the plant. The artists drew every design by hand with pen and ink.

Libbey continued to develop various new product lines for both the retail and foodservice markets. One of the emerging markets in the late 1970s was premium give-a-ways. The give away programs were glassware a customer received as a reward for making another purchase from a convenience store, gas station (Mobil Oil, Sunoco, BP, Shell, Texaco, etc.), or fast food restaurant (Hardee's, McDonalds, or Burger King).

The Red Barn fast food chain started the ball rolling with a red, white, and blue glass decoration in the early 1970s and this was followed by some

Left: [Fig. 5-10] The Drinking Jar was designed in 1990 and originally produced at the Libbey-St.Clair plant in Wallaceburg, Ontario. It became popular around 2013 as the farm-to-table trend grew in popularity.

Facing page: [Fig. 5-11] The tiki cooler was designed by Robert Zollweg in 2016.

other regional chains: Hardee's with Smurfs and Flintstones and Pizza Hut with Care Bears and E.T. With the success of the regional chains, national chains quickly followed. McDonald's 1981 Muppet program was the largest fast food program in Libbey's history with over 41 million pieces, followed by Arby's gold beaded stemware, Coca-Cola bell soda glasses and Tiffany decorations, Burger King with Star Wars, and Long John Silvers with gold beaded stemware.

A number of petroleum companies utilized an array of give away programs, too, such as Shamrock Oil/Valero Oil with Apollo glasses and Shell Oil with NFL logos. Other fuel companies that developed give-away programs featuring Libbey glassware include Mobil Oil, BP Oil, Texaco, Phillips 66, Standard Oil, Esso Corp, and Gulf Oil.

Premium give aways were popular well through the 1990s. The decorating departments flourished in the 1970s and 1980s, the decorating machines ran 24 hours a day, every day of the week in all four decorating locations: Toledo, City of Industry, Shreveport, and Wallaceburg.

The Spuds MacKenzie phenomenon, while it lasted only a few years, was a successful decorated glassware product launch for Libbey. From the first Super Bowl ad in January of 1987 until it was officially retired in late 1989, Libbey sold Spuds glassware to everyone from K-mart to Macy's. Libbey decorated every type of beer glass, along with coffee mugs, ice buckets, and serving trays. Libbey had the Spuds dog in a Santa outfit for Christmas

and on a surf board and under a beach umbrella for summer. The Libbey artists worked with the creative team at Anheuser-Busch nearly non-stop, and rode the wave of Spuds MacKenzie phenomenon. In 1988, for the celebration of Libbey's 100th year in Toledo, Spuds (the actual dog) along with the Spudettes (three women) arrived in a white limousine and attended a downtown riverfront celebration featuring the Temptations. Libbey's then general manager, John Meier, was the event's unofficial master of ceremonies.

In the mid-1980s computers changed the dynamics in art departments throughout the industry. Fewer artists were needed and by the early 1990s, decorated glass in general was on a decline. The artists remained in Toledo, but the actual glass decorating department was moved to the Shreveport plant in November 2002 and subsequently closed in August 2010. All decorating is now sub-contracted to outside decorators, mainly Custom Deco in east Toledo; Moderne Glass, in Aliquippa, Pennsylvania; and Jafe Decorating in Greenville, Ohio.

Right: [Fig. 5-12] Designed in 2003 by Stacey Kerman, the Omega martini glass is made in Toledo.

Far right: [Fig. 5-13] Z-Stem martini glasses were designed in 1999 and are made in Toledo.

Beyond the Factory

Outlet stores have been part of Libbey Glass since the early 1970s. Outlet stores are not designed to compete with national retailers but rather to help Libbey move excess inventory and experiment with new product presentations. Over the years, Libbey added independent outlet stores across the country, peaking at 38 in the mid 1990s. Libbey eventually closed all of them, except those based at a Libbey production facility.

The Toledo store is an exception. Originally based at the Toledo plant on Buckeye Street, Libbey decided to move the factory outlet store to a much larger space at the Erie Street Market in Toledo's warehouse district, in the 1990s. With over 28,000 square feet and twelve employees, it has proved to be a commercial success. After the success of the Toledo store, a newer and much larger store was built in Shreveport on the grounds of the current factory. The new pole barn-style building, located next to the factory on Jewel Road, has over 16,000 square feet and nine full-time employees.

While outlet stores are a great way for the general public to see a wide-array of Libbey's offerings, trade shows are used by manufacturers around the globe to show off their wares to potential commercial clients. Usually lasting three to five days, they are held in large exhibitions halls in major cities, and are a chance for companies to exhibit their products to national and even international buyers. Libbey has been exhibiting at trade shows for decades, including the National Restaurant Show and

Left: [Fig. 5-14] A Bravua glass, designed by Stacey Kerman in 2002 and made in Toledo.

the International Housewares Show.

Libbey has also maintained a permanent showroom in New York City since the late 1940s. Initially located in the Chrysler Building, it now occupies more than 7,500 square feet of space in the New York Merchandise Mart at 41 Madison Avenue. The new showroom opened in the fall of 2015 and has space for product displays for both the foodservice and retail markets. In the spring of 2017, Libbey opened its first Chicago showroom at 325 W. Huron Street. It displays their exclusive foodservice products for the hotel, hospitality, and restaurant trade.

In 2010, drawing inspiration from the Masion Objet show in Paris, the Libbey design team came up with a series of small, mini ceramic plates and glassware items that could be used to serve small portions of food as mini desserts and appetizers on a buffet table. Their inspiration led to one of the most successful product launches Libbey had seen in years. Libbey called the lines Just Desserts, Just Tastings, Just Cocktails, and Just Baking. Two of Libbey's biggest partners were Pier One Imports and Bed, Bath & Beyond, which featured the collection all of their stores in the United States.

Facing page: [Fig. 5-15] In the 2010s Libbey published a series of books, including "Just Desserts" and "Just Tastings," to help market new product lines of the same names.

Above: [Fig. 5-16] The Baker's Basics bakeware collection.

Right: [Fig. 5-17] The Craft Beer collection was designed in 2013 and is made in Toledo. It is another popular design.

Along with all of the glass and ceramic products came the first ever, self-published Libbey cookbooks. Profits soared with the combination of product and cookbooks, which helped tell the story of miniature desserts and appetizers.

Libbey went on to develop seventeen additional cookbooks or entertaining books for everything from desserts to baking, cocktails to craft brews, and many more.

Libbey Today

In July 2013, after 21 years of running the second largest glass company in the world and 43 years with the company, John Meier decided to retire after taking Libbey to new heights and direction. Stephanie Streeter was named CEO, succeeding Meier. She was the first female leader of the company. William Foley was elected chairman of the board.

In 2014, Libbey launched a major manufacturing and product development project, black label technology (BLT). Spearheaded by Terry Hartman, vice president of Engineering, a team of engineers and designers worked for nearly two years to complete this project. The result was the development of a new sophisticated glass blowing machine at the Shreveport plant. It gave Libbey the ability to produce some of the finest stemware in the world, rivaling such competitors as Reidel Glass in Germa-

ny and Luigi Bormioly in Italy. The BLT project cost nearly $40 million, and is one the largest single projects in Libbey's recent history. The first glass produced as a result of BLT started rolling off the forming line in 2016.

Bill Foley, chairman of the board, succeeded Streeter as CEO in 2016. Foley's background in marketing and product development were some of his chief skills and elevating the Libbey brand and new product selection were his top priorities. He advocated change in marketing and product development and pushed for more innovative products.

One the occasion of the company's bicentennial, Foley was CEO, chairman of the board, and general manager of United States and Canada; James Burmeister was CFO; Susan Kovaks, secretary and legal counsel; Klay Huttleson, vice president of E-Commerce; Antoine Jordan, vice president and general manager, Libbey Europe and Asia; and Pablo Villarreal Zavala, vice president and general manager, Libbey Mexico. With roughly 6,600 employees worldwide—2,000 in Toledo and Shreveport, 3,500 in Mexico, 675 in Europe, and 425 in China—Libbey had annual sales in excess of $800 million in 2017.

Facing page: [Fig. 5-18] The Perfect Signature collection.

Below: [Fig. 5-19] The Masters Reserve collection. Like Perfect Signature, Masters Reserve is a result of Libbey's $40 million black label technology initiative of the 2010s.

Below: [Fig. 5-20] The Chemistry bar collection.

Facing page: [Fig. 5-21] The 200th Anniversary serveware collection designed by Robert Zollweg and produced by Alan Iwamura and the Glass Studio at the Toledo Museum of Art. It is inspired by the Modern American series.

Endnotes

1   Quentin R. Skrabec, Jr., *Edward Drummond Libbey, American Glassmaker* (North Carolina: McFarland & Company, Inc, 2011), 20.

2   Ibid, 18.

3   Ibid, 19.

4   Carl U. Fauster, *Libbey Glass Since 1818: Pictorial History and Collector's Guide* (Toledo: Len Beach Press, 1979), 10.

5   Skrabec, *Edward Drummond Libbey*, 25.

6   Fauster, *Libbey Glass Since 1818*, 22.

7   Skrabec, *Edward Drummond Libbey*, 26.

8   Ibid, 24.

9   Ibid, 34.

10   Ibid, 35.

11   Fauster, *Libbey Glass Since 1818*, 25.

12   Jack K. Paquette, *Blowpipes: Northwest Ohio Glassmaking in the Gas Boom of the 1880s* (Xlibris, 2002), 307.

13   Ibid, 311.

14   Skrabec, *Edward Drummond Libbey*, 46.

15   Ibid, 58.

16   Quentin R. Skrabec, Jr., *Michael Owens and the Glass Industry* (Gretna: Pelican Publishing, 2007), 94.

17   Skrabec, *Edward Drummond Libbey*, 13.

18   *Toledo Blade*, Aug. 18, 1888.

19   Ibid.

20   Ibid.

21   Ibid.

22   Ibid.

23   Ibid.

24   Ibid.

25   Ibid.

26   Paquette, *Blowpipes*, 322.

27   Ibid, 323.

28   Ibid.

29   Skrabec, *Michael Owens and the Glass Industry,* 123.

30   Ibid*,* 124.

31   Barbara Floyd, *The Glass City: Toledo and the Industry that Built it* (Ann Arbor: University of Michigan Press, 2015), 29.

32   Skrabec, *Edward Drummond Libbey*, 68.

33   Floyd, *The Glass City,* 28.

34   Skrabec, *Edward Drummond Libbey*, 33.

35   Skrabec, *Michael Owens and the Glass Industry,* 164.

36   Paquette, *Blowpipes*, 326.

37   Skrabec, *Michael Owens and the Glass Industry,* 164.

38   Ibid*,* 165.

39   Floyd, *The Glass City,* 32.

40   Skrabec, *Michael Owens and the Glass Industry,* 166.

41   Skrabec, *Edward Drummond Libbey*, 85.

42   Skrabec, *Michael Owens and the Glass Industry,* 165.

43   Floyd, *The Glass City,* 30.

44   Skrabec, *Edward Drummond Libbey*, 86.

45   Floyd, *The Glass City,* 32.

46   Skrabec, *Michael Owens and the Glass Industry*, 165.

47   Skrabec, *Edward Drummond Libbey*, 87.

48   Skrabec, *Michael Owens and the Glass Industry,* 167.

49   Ibid, 167.

50   Skrabec, *Edward Drummond Libbey*, 88.

51   Skrabec, *Michael Owens and the Glass Industry,* 171.

52   Ibid, 172.

53   Floyd, *The Glass City,* 44.

54   Skrabec, *Michael Owens and the Glass Industry,* 178.

55   Skrabec, *Edward Drummond Libbey*, 7.

56   LaShelle, Darren, and Richard Wells, "Old West End Tour," Toledo's Attic (Toledo's Attic Essay, 1997).

57   Floyd, *The Glass City*, 36.

58   Skrabec, *Edward Drummond Libbey*, 115-116.

59   Ibid, 116.

60   Julie A. McMaster, The Enduring Legacy: A Pictorial History of the Toledo Museum of Art (Toledo, OH. Toledo Museum of Art, 2001), 10.

61   Ibid, 12.

62   Skrabec, *Edward Drummond Libbey,* 121.

63   McMaster, *The Enduring Legacy,* 13.

64   Skrabec, *Edward Drummond Libbey,* 129.

65   Ibid, 129.

66   Ibid, 137.

67   McMaster, *The Enduring Legacy,* 16.

68   Ibid, 17.

69   Volongo, Sally "Pavilion is just the latest addition to a growing art museum campus." *The Blade* (Toledo, OH), August 20, 2006.

70   Skrabec, *Edward Drummond Libbey,* 155.

71   McMaster, *The Enduring Legacy,* 26.

72   Ibid, 26.

73   Ibid, 26.

74   Ibid, 28.

75   Ibid, 29.

76   Ibid, 29.

77   Corning Museum of Glass, "The Fabulous Monster: Owens Bottle Machine," Corning Museum of Glass Research, (Corning Museum of Glass, Oct. 2011).

78   Ibid.

79   Paquette, *Blowpipes*, 361.

80   Ibid, 345.

81   Beiser, Vince, "How The Owens Bottle Company Helped End American Child Labor," *Pacific Standard*, Aug. 6, 2018.

82   Paquette, *Blowpipes*, 365.

83   "Time in a Bottle: A History of Owens-Illinois, Inc.," Ward M. Canaday Center for Special Collectionas, University of Toledo, (June 2006).

84   Paquette, *Blowpipes*, 331.

85   "Time in a Bottle: A History of Owens-Illinois, Inc.," Ward M. Can-

aday Center for Special Collectionas, University of Toledo, (June 2006).

86   Floyd, *The Glass City,* 67.

87   Ibid, 68.

88   Parker, Kevin, "Flat-Glass Making Thrives in Toledo," *Processing: Solutions for the Process Industries* (Jan. 2015).

89   Scott, Virginia, "The Libbey Glass Company Part 3: The Libbey-Nash Series," Glass Review (National Depression Glass Association, Nov. 1978.)

90   "For the bride: Libbey's Monticello Glassware," Corning Museum of Glass, (May 2017).

91   Fauster, Carl, "Mid-Twentieth Century Expansion Years, 1943-1968," Libbey Glass Since 1818, (Len Beach Press, 1979) 134.

92   "Huge Glass Plant Formally Opened," *Los Angeles Times*, Oct. 7, 1962.

93   Ibid.

94   Paquette, Jack, "The Glassmaskers, Revisted," (Bloomington: Xlibris, 2010).

95   "LOF Plans To Shut Down Local Plant," *The Times*, (Shreveport, Louisiana), Mar. 9, 1971.

96   Duncan, Debra, "Glass museum would honor Mount Pleasant's productive past," *Pittsburg-Post Gazette*, Jan. 17, 2013.

97   "New glass firm in Wallaceburg," *The Windsor Star*, Sept. 20, 1978, 5.

98   "Owens Plans Sale of its Glass Tableware Unit," *The New York Times*, Apr. 24, 1993, national edition, sec. 1, 39.

99   Saari, Malia, "Town's main plant may close," *The Windsor Star*, Jan. 5, 1999, 5.

100   "Libbey to Close California Factory," *Toledo Blade*, Aug. 17, 2004.

Selected Bibliography

Beiser, Vince. "How The Owens Bottle Company Helped End American Child Labor," *Pacific Standard*, August 6, 2018.

Duncan, Debra. "Glass museum would honor Mount Pleasant's productive past," *Pittsburg-Post Gazette*, January 17, 2013.

Fauster, Carl U. *Libbey Glass Since 1818: Pictorial History & Collectors Guide*. Toledo, OH: Len Beach Press, 1979.

Floyd, Barbara L. *The Glass City: Toledo and the Industry That Built It*. Ann Arbor, MI: University of Michigan Press, 2015.

McMaster, Julie. *The Enduring Legacy: A Pictorial History of the Toledo Museum of Art*. Toledo, OH: Toledo Museum of Art, 2001.

Paquette, Jack K. *Blowpipes: Northwest Ohio Glassmaking in the Gas Boom of the 1880s*. Bloomington: Xlibris, 2002.

_____. "The Glassmakers, Revisited," Bloomington: Xlibris, 2010.

Parker, Kevin. "Flat-Glass Making Thrives in Toledo," *Processing: Solutions for the Process Industries*. January 2015.

Saari, Malia. "Town's main plant may close," *The Windsor Star*, January 5, 1999.

Scott, Virginia. "The Libbey Glass Company Part 3: The Libbey-Nash Series," *Glass Review*. National Depression Glass Association, November 1978.

Skrabec, Quentin R., Jr. *Michael Owens and the Glass Industry*. Gretna, LA: Pelican Publishing, 2007.

_____. *Glass in Northwest Ohio*. Charleston, SC: Arcadia Publishing, 2007.

_____. *Edward Drummond Libbey, American Glassmaker*. Jefferson, NC: McFarland & Company, Inc., Publishers, 2011.

Volongo, Sally. "Pavilion is just the latest addition to a growing art museum campus," *The Blade*. Toledo, OH: August 20, 2006.

Index

Photo Credits

Special thanks to all of the listed organizations and individuals for allowing the reproduction of the listed photos. Their cooperation was invaluable and is greatly appreciated.

Portraits

Page 7: Deming Jarves (1790-1869), Oil on canvas, Artist Unknown. Museum Accession No. 1983.45, a gift from the great-granddaughter of Deming Jarves. Courtesy of the Sandwich Glass Museum. **Page 9**: William L. Libbey. Photo courtesy The Toledo Museum of Art. **Page 33**: Edward D. Libbey. Photo courtesy The Toledo Museum of Art. **Page 45**: Michael J. Owens. Photo courtesy The Toledo-Lucas County Public Library, Images in Time. **Page 62**: Edwin W. Fuerst. Photo courtesy The Toledo Museum of Art.

Photos

Fig. 1-1: Photo courtesy The Toledo Museum of Art. **Fig. 1-2**: Accession number 2010.4.13, Collection of The Corning Museum of Glass, Corning, NY. **Fig. 1-3**: Accession number 2004.4.63, Collection of The Corning Museum of Glass, Corning, NY. **Fig. 1-4:** Accession number 93.4.87, Collection of The Corning Museum of Glass, Corning, NY. **Fig. 1-5:** Accession number 93.4.9, Collection of The Corning Museum of Glass, Corning, NY. **Fig. 1-6:** Object number 1951.202, Collection of The Toledo Museum of Art, gift of Owens-Illinois Glass Company. **Fig. 1-7:** Object number 1974.52, Collection of The Toledo Museum of Art, purchased with funds from the Libbey Endowment, Gift of Edward Drummond Libbey. **Fig. 1-8:** Accession number 90.4.170, Collection of The Corning Museum of Glass, Corning, NY. Gift of Harriet Smith. **Fig. 1-9:** Object number 1951.203, Collection of The Toledo Museum of Art, gift of Owens-Illinois Glass Company. **Fig. 1-10:** Object number 1958.68, Collection of The Toledo Museum of Art, gift of Marie W. Greenhalgh in memory of her parents, Alice Libbey Walbridge and William S. Walbridge. **Fig. 1-11:** Object number 1968.8, Collection of The Toledo Museum of Art, purchased with funds from the Libbey Endowment, Gift of Edward Drummond Libbey. **Fig. 1-13, Fig. 1-14, Fig. 1-15, Fig. 1-16,** and **Fig. 1-17:** Photos courtesy The Toledo Museum of Art, from the Collection of William H. Rice, gift of Sally and James Crocker. **Fig. 1-18:** Object number 1951.2, The Toledo Museum of Art, gift of Owens-Illinois Glass Company. **Fig. 1-19:** Photo courtesy The University of Toledo Ward M. Canaday Center. **Fig. 1-20:** Object number 1958.52, Collection of The Toledo Museum of Art, gift of Marie W. Greenhalgh in memory of her parents, Alice Libbey Walbridge and William S. Walbridge. **Fig. 1-21, Fig. 1-22, Fig. 1-23,** and **Fig. 1-24:** Photos courtesy The Toledo Museum of Art. **Fig. 1-25:** Photo courtesy The Toledo-Lucas County Public Library, Images in Time. **Fig. 1-26, Fig. 1-27, Fig. 1-28,** and **Fig. 1-29:** Photos courtesy The Toledo Museum of Art. **Fig. 1-30, Fig. 1-31,** and **Fig. 1-32:** Photos courtesy Vance Hall.

Fig. **2-1** and **Fig. 2-2:** Photo courtesy The Toledo Museum of Art. **Fig. 2-4:** Photo courtesy The Toledo-Lucas County Public Library, Images in Time. **Fig. 2-5** and **Fig. 2-6:** Photos courtesy the Ojai Valley Museum. **Fig. 2-7:** Photo courtesy The Toledo Museum of Art.

Fig. **3-1:** Photo courtesy The University of Toledo Ward M. Canaday Center. **Fig. 3-2:** Object number 1951.266, Collection of The Toledo Museum of Art, gift of Owens-Illinois Glass Company. **Fig. 3-3:** Photo courtesy The Toledo Museum of Art. **Fig. 3-4:** Reproduced with permission. *Scientific American*, April 30, 1904. **Fig. 3-5, Fig. 3-6, Fig. 3-7, Fig. 3-8, Fig. 3-9,** and **Fig. 3-10:** Photo courtesy The University of Toledo Ward M. Canaday Center. **Fig. 3-11** and **Fig. 3-12:** Photo courtesy the Toledo Museum of Art. **Fig. 3-13:** Photo courtesy The Toledo-Lucas County Public Library, Images in Time. **Fig. 3-14:** Object number 1969.84, Collection of The Toledo Museum of Art, gift of Owens-Illinois, Inc. **Fig. 3-15:** Object number 1979.50, Collection of The Toledo

Museum of Art, gift of Marilyn M. Logan in memory of Richard D. Logan, Jr. **Fig. 3-16:** Object number 1983.89, Collection of The Toledo Museum of Art, gift of Jane DeVilbiss Shuey. **Fig. 3-17:** Photo courtesy The University of Toledo Ward M. Canaday Center. **Fig. 3-18:** Object number 1951.170, Collection of The Toledo Museum of Art, gift of Owens-Illinois Glass Company. **Fig. 3-19:** Object number 2005.70, Collection of The Toledo Museum of Art, bequest of Edwin D. Dodd. **Fig. 3-20:** Object number 2005.26, Collection of The Toledo Museum of Art, gift of Art St. John. **Fig. 3-21:** Photo courtesy The Toledo-Lucas County Public Library, Images in Time. **Fig. 3-22:** Object number 1968.59A, Collection of The Toledo Museum of Art, gift of Mrs. Carl R. Megowen in memory of Carl R. Megowen. **Fig. 3-23:** Object number 2005.69, Collection of The Toledo Museum of Art, bequest of Edwin D. Dodd. **Fig. 3-24:** Object number 2005.73, Collection of The Toledo Museum of Art, bequest of Edwin D. Dodd. **Fig. 3-25:** Object number 2005.64, Collection of The Toledo Museum of Art, bequest of Edwin D. Dodd. **Fig. 3-26:** Photo courtesy The Toledo Museum of Art. **Fig. 3-27:** Object number 1969.28, Collection of The Toledo Museum of Art, gift of Owens-Illinois, Inc. **Fig. 3-28:** Object number 2004.33, Collection of The Toledo Museum of Art, gift of H. Charles Yaeger. **Fig. 3-29, Fig. 3-30, Fig. 3-31, Fig. 3-32,** and **Fig. 3-33:** Photos courtesy The Toledo Museum of Art. **Fig. 3-34:** Object number 2012.87, Collection of The Toledo Museum of Art, gift of Libbey Glass, Inc. **Fig. 3-35** and **Fig. 3-36:** Photos courtesy of Libbey Inc. **Fig.**

3-37, **Fig. 3-38,** and **Fig. 3-39:** Photos courtesy The Kentucky Derby Museum.

Fig. 4-1: Photo courtesy The University of Toledo Ward M. Canaday Center. **Fig. 4-3:** Photo courtesy of the Wallaceburg and District Museum. **Fig. 4-4** and **Fig. 4-5:** Photos courtesy Libbey Inc. **Fig. 4-7, Fig. 4-8,** and **Fig. 4-9:** Photos courtesy The Onondaga Historical Association. **Fig. 4-10** through **Fig. 4-15:** Photos courtesy Libbey Inc.

Fig. 5-1 through **Fig. 5-21:** Photos courtesy Libbey Inc.